The Healing Names of Jesus invites readers to interact with the multifaceted ways in which Jesus brings healing to our lives. One size does not fit all! Combining serious Bible study with real-life examples (many of which are personal), Jenita ultimately points readers to Jesus, our all-sufficient healer. Her desire for readers to experience healing comes through every page of the book.

Bryan Beyer
Bible Professor Emeritus
Columbia International University, Columbia, SC

With wisdom born of pain from her own story, Jenita has written an essential devotional that reminds us of Jesus' ability to heal our deepest wounds and restore us. She bravely shares the fear that gripped her heart and how that same fear would give way to a far greater power: the healing name of Jesus.

Julie Hull
MA, Pastoral Counselor
Renewing Hope Counseling and Coaching, Minneapolis, MN

From the opening sentences of the introduction and throughout every page, Jenita courageously opens a door, inviting us into her personal journey through depression and anxiety. By wrapping biblical discoveries, personal examples, and practical applications together, Jenita guides the reader toward a deeper understanding of the One who brings true healing. This book is one that needs to be read with a Bible in one hand and a journal in the other, with the expectation that Jesus will meet you right where you are and provide strength and peace for the journey. Thank you, Jenita!

Reverend Mike Richards
Senior Pastor
CrossPoint Church, Bloomington, MN

For those who struggle with mental illness, particularly anxiety and depression, the battle often seems hopeless and solitary. Author Jenita Pace dispels such lies in *The Healing Names of Jesus*. There is hope, and those who suffer are not alone. Jenita draws earthly parallels to the names of God and shares her personal struggles with mental illness, explaining how God's Word and character, as revealed through his names, have transformed her mind and heart. The book's impact is found in its transparency and sincere belief in a God who has been with her through all her struggles and who will be with readers in their struggles too. I can further testify that this book is a true reflection of her character, her love for her Lord, and her love for those who suffer. I wholeheartedly recommend it in our ministry.

Julie Andersen
Care Director
New Hope Church, New Hope, MN

When it comes to mental health, too many books offer optimistic assurances beyond that which can be realistically promised. In *The Healing Names of Jesus*, however, author Jenita Pace not only guides readers on a journey that balances hope in God with hope in the readers themselves, but she also illustrates the powers of vulnerability and faith within the paradoxical process of suffering and healing. Her writing masterfully harmonizes challenge with compassion, weakness with strength, and vulnerability with courage. This book can undoubtedly encourage and embolden everyone who reads it.

Mark E. Anderson
Psychologist
New Brighton, MN

If you or someone you love struggles with depression or anxiety, this book is the faithful friend you have been searching for. *The Healing Names of Jesus* goes far beyond simple devotions; it boldly ushers us into the presence of God. In its pages, author Jenita Pace personally intercedes on behalf of the reader and invites them in a most loving, compassionate way to confront the kinds of suffering that few are willing to admit or address, ultimately connecting them to the profound hope found in Jesus' character. Save yourself and those you love from loneliness and despair by reading, absorbing, and passing this book along to others so that you may refresh others as you, too, are refreshed.

Reverend Colin P. Thornley
Mentoring Specialist
Serge Global, Inc., Arden, NC

The Healing Names of Jesus is a must-have resource for anyone trapped in the fog of depression and anxiety and in search of comfort and light, and it is written from the heart of someone who has personally survived. Jenita Pace's approach to healing lends structure and asks questions, making the content both personal and applicable. Pastors, counselors, chaplains, friends, and family members will gain insight into the lives and challenges of those who struggle with mental health and learn to ask meaningful questions that will deepen their interactions with the people they love.

Glen Bloomstrom, Chaplain (Colonel) Retired, US Army
M.Div., MA, MSS, Director, Faith Community Engagement
LivingWorks Education, Minneapolis, MN

THE HEALING NAMES OF JESUS

Find Freedom
from Depression
and Anxiety

JENITA PACE, LPC

BroadStreet
PUBLISHING

BroadStreet Publishing® Group, LLC
Savage, Minnesota, USA
BroadStreetPublishing.com

The Healing Names of Jesus: Find Freedom from Depression and Anxiety
Copyright © 2021 Jenita Pace

978-1-4245-6276-3 (hardcover)
978-1-4245-6277-0 (e-book)

Stock or custom editions of BroadStreet Publishing titles may be purchased in bulk for educational, business, ministry, fundraising, or sales promotional use. For information, please email orders@broadstreetpublishing.com.

Design and typesetting | garborgdesign.com

Printed in China

21 22 23 24 25 5 4 3 2 1

This book is dedicated to Timothy Nathan Pace,
a man who beautifully lives for others
because of his love for Jesus.

You have saved me in every way
that a person can save another.

Love you.

CONTENTS

INTRODUCTION

I have prayed for you. We have never met, but I imagine that if you chose to read this book and come along this journey, depression and anxiety have affected you in some way. Depression and anxiety aren't experiences that everyone necessarily understands, but for those who do, these common enemies tend to draw people together. Naturally, I feel a special bond with people who have endured the same struggles I have.

My personal journey began in 2001, when I found myself sleeping nearly all of the time, struggling to focus, feeling sad and constantly afraid, and avoiding people to hide my pain. I hated getting out of bed. I hated leaving my house, and I felt stuck.

At the time, my husband, Tim, was a pastor at a small church and finishing his pastoral degree. I felt the need to be a "good Christian" and support him in his role. But the more depressed I became, the more I skipped church and the more worthless I felt. It was even more embarrassing and shameful when the lead pastor confronted Tim about my "inability to support the church."

I began to believe a dangerous lie: Tim would be better off without me. Perhaps you, too, can relate to this feeling of worthlessness. Not only did this powerful, disabling lie lead me to believe that I was not earning my keep as a spouse and that I was a failure, but it also had me convinced that I would never find my way out of the dark hole that held my mind prisoner.

I decided I would kill myself. I would execute my carefully crafted plan while Tim was at church. After he said goodbye and left, I laid out the medications I intended to use to overdose and wrote a letter to Tim explaining why everything would be better if I were no longer here on earth with him. But as it happened, Tim forgot his pager at home (yes, this was a long time ago!) and had turned the car around to come home and retrieve it. When he walked into the house, I panicked and quickly tried to cover up what I had been doing, but it was too late. He started to cry, and I did too. It was a moment of true heartbreak.

Tim brought me to the hospital that night, and I was admitted against my will. I found myself scared and alone. All of my personal belongings were taken from me except my clothes and my Bible. Unable to sleep, I frantically flipped through my Bible in search of no particular verse when I stumbled on Psalm 121:

> I lift up my eyes to the mountains—
> where does my help come from?
> My help comes from the LORD,
> the Maker of heaven and earth.
> He will not let your foot slip—
> he who watches over you will not slumber;
> indeed, he who watches over Israel
> will neither slumber nor sleep.
> The LORD watches over you—
> the LORD is your shade at your right hand;
> the sun will not harm you by day,
> nor the moon by night.
> The LORD will keep you from all harm—
> he will watch over your life;
> the LORD will watch over your coming and going
> both now and forevermore. (NIV)

The words were like salve on a wound. Over the course of the ten days that followed, I read this psalm morning, noon, and night. I clung to it despite my confusion: *Why would God allow this to happen to me? What good could possibly come from this?*

Once I was released from the hospital, I checked my voicemail to find it full of messages from people who were praying for me. One was from Steve Bradley, a professor at the Christian university from which I had graduated. In his voicemail, Steve said, "Jenita, I couldn't sleep last night. I was thinking about you. I don't know why, but I felt like I needed to read Psalm 121." Tears spilled from my eyes. Perhaps God hadn't abandoned me after all.

Steve asked if I would meet his wife, Pat. I admit I was hesitant. All of my well-meaning friends had brought me books and Scripture cards to encourage me, but I found them discouraging—mostly because I couldn't comprehend much at the time. Some viewed my depression as proof of sin or a lack of faith, but Pat had been through depression years ago on the mission field and saw no shame in experiencing it.

Full of unconditional love and support, Pat came to my home and told me about her own battles with depression. She called me in the mornings, and if I wasn't out of bed, then she would come over and help me get up and moving. She often brought food and sometimes stopped by just to pray, listen, and offer comfort. She understood that I was hopeless and promised to hold on to hope for me so that I wouldn't lose it entirely. She constantly promised me, "Jenita, God will use this. You will see."

About a month after my first meeting with Pat, Tim called me from work, obviously shaken. He told me Pat had died suddenly in her sleep from an aneurism. Devastated, I cried hysterically as questions raced through my mind: *Why would God take away the one person who seemed to understand?* I desperately needed a distraction and decided to go for a walk to get the mail. Our mailbox was one block away, so I clumsily put on my shoes and started down our busy street. We were living in a housing community for married students, and the joyful sounds of children playing and neighbors visiting buzzed all around me. I felt numb to all of it.

Tears blurred my vision as I opened our mailbox and gathered its contents. I shuffled through the mail then abruptly stopped. In my hands was a card from Pat. I frantically tore open the envelope and read the simple note she had left inside: "Jenita, I wanted to write this down so that you won't forget: God will use this. You will see."

In utter shock, I stood in the street and read Pat's words over and over again. I cried from both the weight of my grief and the encouragement I found in her words. My dear friend, beyond her death, left me with the hope I needed to keep going.

A counselor suggested that Tim move me home to Minnesota, where my family could support both him and me, so we packed up our belongings and moved. I attended individual counseling, met with therapy groups, and received spiritual mentorship. The more I understood God, the less power depression and anxiety had over me and my life. Gradually, both afflictions lost their power altogether. I found freedom from the thoughts that imprisoned me, and I even discovered my passion for helping others. Now I am grateful to say that I am a licensed professional counselor with a private practice in Minnesota.

The inspiration for the development of this book was the lessons I had learned from my personal experience, primarily that our dark thoughts and feelings lose their grip when we understand God. He uses so many names and metaphors to help us know him. He's multidimensional: three separate persons in one God. He calls himself the Father, the Son, and the Holy Spirit. Each person in the Trinity joins with the others to create a perfect wholeness that makes God, and each dimension offers a glimpse into who he is and how he feels about us. It's a paradox that is difficult to understand but an essential part of the journey to healing. The more we recognize him in and around us, the more powerful our hope, faith, and strength grow.

Therefore, as we take time through the following lessons to look at each characteristic and name of God, we will identify which part of the Trinity the names represent. Some characteristics and names can be representative of all three, so to identify the person we are discussing, I will use the following symbols:

Father

Son

Spirit

As you learn more about each person, you will come to understand why these symbols align with what we know about each one. Then, after you have read about the background for each name, I invite you to engage in an activity that brings the concept to life and offer a closing prayer.

Here are a few additional tips for how to maximize our time together through this study. First, read each day's Scripture verses, which appear below each day's title. I recommend taking your time reading each one and highlighting or underlining any words or phrases that stand out to you. Some verses appear more than once because God sometimes expresses multiple metaphors and names for himself within the same passage. When rereading Scripture that was previously covered, read them from a fresh perspective and look for new insight. Some of the Scripture readings may be long, but please do not cheat yourself of the richness of God's Word!

Second, you will want a journal for many of the activities, which will require paper and a writing utensil. I further recommend tracking your thoughts and emotions in writing throughout your journey. It will be helpful and encouraging to look back and see how your transformation unfolded.

Third, take time to pray. Prayer does not require a specific format; prayer is a conversation with our Lord. Discard any formulas for prayer and simply say to him whatever you feel. Keep talking to God even if you're fed up, angry, and only have curse words for him. He can handle it, and his deepest desire is to be with you.

Lastly, I encourage you to contact a friend or pastor or even to form a small group with whom you can journey through this book. God exists in community, and if God desires community, then we certainly should as well. If you prefer to do this privately, that is okay, but I highly recommend someone join you.

I am honored and humbled to be on this journey with you, and my hope—my passion—is that *you* find hope. And if you don't have hope, then let me carry it for you! As your understanding of God broadens and you see him as he is, hope will color your surroundings every day.

Jenita Pace

The Lamb and the Shepherd

I remember visiting my son's preschool class on the same day they were expecting a special visitor: a farmer who brought a lamb from her local farm. The sight of my son and his little classmates enjoying the presence of a baby animal was precious. This sweet, innocent little creature was surprisingly trusting.

Sheep are vulnerable animals. With no way to defend themselves, they live in a perpetual state of alertness, using their herd to help them detect danger. The problem with this setup is that sheep scare easily. When one scares, they all seem to scare.[1] Another major handicap that sheep face is their poor depth perception. They can see all the way around themselves, but they can't distinguish objects that are far away, and they can't judge the distance between themselves and the perceived danger.[2] Therefore, the sheep's philosophy is to assume that everything is dangerous, just to be safe.

Sheep are also emotional creatures. They seek connection and develop friendships within their herd. Much like dogs, sheep recognize and distinguish voices and mannerisms among people. Sheep also develop trust and connection with their shepherd if he or she spends enough time with them. Each sheep has its unique personality, and they are just as diverse as human personalities. Living in a herd is not an indication of stupidity; it's a necessity for their survival. They need each other.[3]

Our almighty God came to earth in the metaphor of a lamb in Isaiah 53:7: "He was brought like a gentle lamb to be slaughtered" (TPT). And not just any lamb but one that would be despised, rejected, unattractive, and familiar with suffering and pain. He would be someone that even his herd would reject. What a terrifying concept for a little lamb in a flock!

We know from the story in the New Testament that Jesus did come to earth, just as Isaiah prophesied. And his life unfolded as Isaiah predicted. Jesus chose to be defenseless and vulnerable, and in return, he was hated, rejected, unloved by many, convicted of crimes he didn't commit, and eventually murdered. Because of his decision to take on this vulnerable role as a little lamb, he now has the power as our Shepherd to understand what it's like to be in our herd and be vulnerable and scared. The night before he was arrested and later crucified, Jesus openly displayed fear and cried out to his Father. Thank you, Jesus, for showing us how much you understand what it is like to feel alone and afraid!

Isaiah described Jesus as the innocent and vulnerable lamb, and Jesus described himself as the "good Shepherd" (John 10:11). Further, Jesus defined a good shepherd: the good Shepherd calls his sheep by their individual names, leads them, defends them from predators, emotionally cares about them, and is willing to die for them. He knows what it means to be part of the flock, so he truly is the best kind of shepherd.

Sheep require constant protection, which meant that shepherds watched their flocks day and night. Without a guardian, the animals were simply unsafe. Herds grazed far from villages in biblical times, which meant that shepherds had to be alert and on guard against lions, bears, and jackals. For this reason, shepherds often carried two weapons: a club (called a rod) and a sling shot. The rod allowed shepherds to defend their sheep at close range, and the sling shot could be used against predators at a distance. The sling shot could also be used to get the attention of any wandering sheep.[4] Shepherds carried staffs, which were not used as weapons but tools to track and guide sheep through narrow passages. If one sheep strayed too far, the shepherd beckoned it to come back.

At night, shepherds were responsible for bringing the sheep someplace safe, where they would be protected from predators or thieves. Naturally, the most vulnerable members among the flock were the little lambs. Every morning, a shepherd counted the entire flock as they left their safe place, and he recounted when they returned to safety each night.[5] If any member went missing, then the shepherd searched for it; even one missing sheep meant the shepherd could be held liable to the herd's owner.[6]

Another disadvantage that sheep must contend with is their generally weak immunity. They get sick easily, and when they do, they tend to hide their symptoms, knowing that weakness makes them vulnerable.[7] This meant that shepherds had to be observant, watching each one carefully and carrying any member of the flock who was unable to keep up.[8] Because of the demands of the job, the shepherd spent an incredible amount of time with the flock and truly got to know them as individuals.

What an incredible calling to be the guardian and protector of one of the most vulnerable animals in the world, and not just any animal but one acutely aware of its inability to protect itself and is therefore skittish. I relate easily to the metaphor of sheep. I tend to panic first and ask questions later. When I sense danger, it is difficult to stop fear from soaking into my heart and leaving me in a state of panic. My heart seems to have poor depth perception. That is, I can't anticipate the future, and that terrifies me.

If you are anxious and fear the unknown, then I want you to be able to hear your good Shepherd calling you by name, holding your hand as he guides you through times of uncertainty or danger, trusting that he defends your soul from Satan, believing that he intimately understands your pain—all the while knowing that he died in order to lead you. Even if you stray, he is committed to finding you and will search for you.

Like sheep, we may be tempted to hide our weaknesses and illnesses, but he sees them and wants to be our caregiver. When you feel you cannot go on, he will tenderly carry you. And if you feel forgotten, unwelcome, or rejected by the flock, he understands. The Great Shepherd closely watches the ones who are most vulnerable, keeping his weapons near to defend his flock against the enemy. He is more than capable of fighting off predators and will not allow the great thief to steal you from him.

Meditate on the times in your past when you felt scared and your Shepherd led you through the danger. Even though you were afraid, he called you by name and guided you. Draw near to him. He keeps watch over you.

Bring It to Life

- Read Psalm 23. David, the author, spent years as a shepherd. I even recommend writing this passage out in your journal, underlining all the verbs that pertain to what Jesus does as our Shepherd. What do you notice?

- What is your "darkest valley"? What makes it so scary? Note the dark valleys through which your Shepherd has already led you. How did he do it? Whom did he use? What did he do?

- Close your eyes and meditate on the picture of green pastures and quiet waters. Look at images or visit a place that represents this for you. The darkest valleys are part of the journey, but you can mentally and emotionally rest in those safe places next to your Shepherd, who calls you by name.

Jesus, my Shepherd, you came as one of us, the most vulnerable version of us. I pray to you, Shepherd, as I walk through this scary valley. You know the danger; you have seen each day ahead of us, and you have already walked it. I pray to really see you guiding me to a safe place in my mind and to hear you whispering my name. I pray for green pastures and still waters, where I can rest mentally, knowing you have already mapped out each day.

DAY 2

Lion of Judah

GENESIS 44; REVELATION 5:5; PROVERBS 28:1

Male lions are magnificent animals. Weighing as much as five hundred pounds and reaching up to ten feet in length, they are truly impressive in appearance and strength. At their top speed, lions can run in bursts up to forty miles per hour and leap thirty-six feet.[9]

But it is not just their incredible strength that sets them apart from other animals. Lions are uniquely family oriented. While other big cats tend to live solitary lives, lions are extremely sociable and live within family units called "prides." Prides are the definition of community, with members living together and depending on each other for survival. The lionesses are in charge of raising the young and hunting while the male lion guards the borders of the family's territory and provide protection from predators and competing male lions, who would kill the cubs.[10]

Even in the darkest night, the defender of the family can secure their safety. His eyes have internal mirrors of sorts, which take the light and reflect it to maximize his eyesight and allow him to patrol day and night. With razor sharp teeth and massive claws, he is truly a terrifying defender of his family.[11]

And he is always close at hand. The roar of a lion can carry up to five miles. It's an intimidating sound but one that brings comfort and reassurance to the pride.[12]

God has chosen this metaphor for himself along with the name of Judah. Judah, the brave intercessor in Genesis 44, offers to take the punishment in place of his brother, Benjamin, on account of his love for his father. How absolutely fitting: our Savior is the mighty lion who courageously fought to keep us, his family, safe.

This is the name of Jesus that most brings me comfort when I am anxious and afraid. Afraid of other people, afraid of circumstances I can't control in my life, afraid of something happening to me or my family, afraid the internal darkness I wrestle with will overwhelm me, afraid of all of the unknowns in my future. And research shows that fear gains ground when we feel a sense of powerlessness. The less power we feel over a situation, the more intense our fears become.[13] Can you relate?

Each of us faces specific internal fears that maybe others do not face. For me, perfectionism is a continual battle: the feeling that I am never good enough. It is the fear that I can't do things well enough or that I simply can't *be* enough. This nightmare came true when I worked for a woman who was particularly difficult to please. She had no tolerance for errors. If I stepped away from my desk, I would return to find notes and printouts showing things I had done wrong, wanting explanations for my errors, and demanding discussions on how to avoid mistakes in the future. If I had a question, it was typical for her to refuse to answer. She wanted me to figure it out for myself. I remember being so afraid each day of making a mistake, not sure what to do if I needed help.

The situation grew more tense when I suddenly had a seizure and had to go on epilepsy medication, which made it difficult to focus. My supervisor was not shy about making it clear that she was working to develop a case to let me go. She would ask me to print out any mistakes I made and to deliver them to her office so she could file them in a drawer while I watched. It was a perfectionist's nightmare.

I was able to get a new job in which I thrived. However, I noticed that I now had more anxiety and doubts about myself and my abilities. The anxiety surfaced every time I started a project, had to collaborate with others, took a leadership role, or started working with a new client.

Years later, I was participating in a training program to learn a therapeutic intervention called Eye Movement Desensitization Reprocessing (EMDR). EMDR is an excellent tool for someone plagued by a fear that is holding their mental health hostage. The process begins by having the participant return to a core memory when that fear was most realized. I know the fear of failure holds a lot of power in my life, so I decided to focus on overcoming that challenge. As the process began, my mind brought me back to a moment at my job when I had in my hand a printout of an error I had made. My supervisor took the printout from me, walked to her desk, and filed it in a drawer.

As I processed that memory, which had filled me with fear, failure, and disappointment, it began to shift. I suddenly saw a lion standing between the supervisor and me. He was huge and calm. He looked not at her but instead kept his kind, focused eyes on me. And he had purposely placed his body directly between her and me.

In that moment, instead of seeing myself as powerless, I realized the Lion of Judah protected me. I had not been alone. I falsely assumed that my supervisor had the power to change the course of my life, but the truth was that God was in the position of power over every aspect of that experience. He knew that I would leave that position and that I was on the road to becoming a therapist. He never wanted my supervisor's evaluation of me to become my lifelong evaluation of myself.

I still struggle at times with fears of failure. Perfectionism is a particular fear that can uniquely fuel depression, and it is gaining momentum in society. It can be difficult to pinpoint because sometimes it gets confused with having high standards.[14] High standards aren't harmful, but if you are intensely afraid of not being the best or of not doing well and your identity is tied to your success, let the Lion of Judah drive those feelings from your mind!

Other fears have presented themselves to me: some of them physical dangers, financial challenges, emotional hardships, and mental struggles. The intensity of my fear can feel extremely overwhelming. The pressure intensifies when I feel powerless, and sometimes the amount of control I have is limited.

But then I turn and see this great Lion of Judah: the One who can see even in the darkest of nights, who knows the borders of my mind and my heart and can guard me from the enemy. His courage can fill me up, live within me, and shine through me. He can do that for you too.

Bring It to Life

- Draw a circle and write your name inside of it. Then write traits that describe you inside the circle as well. For example, I included the words *hospitable*, *humorous*, and *creative*.

- Outside of the circle, write down some of the things that threaten your mental and emotional safety, such as perfectionism, fear, grief, doubt, and so on.

- Picture the Lion of Judah, walking the border of your circle. Is there one threat in particular that scares you more than the others? What is it, and why is it more threatening?

- Ntwadumela (a name that means "one who greets with fire") was the star lion in a 2006 National Geographic documentary. He became internationally known because he exhibited so much passion in keeping his pride safe. I recommend watching videos of him on YouTube or purchasing the documentary, called *Eternal Enemies: Lions and Hyenas*.

Our Lion of Judah, the protector of my mental and emotional borders, please guard my mind and heart and spirit today. Keep them safe from the things that hunt me, whether something emotional, mental, or physical. Jesus, I know you long to rescue each of us, to keep us safe from the dangers of this world. Please, I pray that whatever my deepest fear is right now, confront it and bring me to a place where I really feel your protection in my heart. Lion of Judah, in my memories, show me of times when you were there, guarding me in ways I didn't even know.

Son of Man

✝

ISAIAH 53:3–5; LUKE 19:1–10;
2 CORINTHIANS 1:1–7; PSALM 34:18

Jesus referred to himself as the Son of Man. To call himself the son of a human seems a bit obvious, but it is such a powerful name with a beautiful application. For one thing, the title implies that in taking on human flesh, Jesus also embraced human suffering.

The concept of suffering is one that haunts and scares us. I have had clients ask me to assure them that life will get better, that the pain is in the past, and they want me to promise them that the future is bright and beautiful. I can't offer that. The world around us is too unpredictable. Instead of helping you chase a life of comfort and safety, where no harm befalls you, I want to help you find comfort and safety *inside* you, comfort and safety that can't be stolen from you.

When we talk about what Jesus did for us, the conversation usually centers around the horrible death he endured in order to have a relationship with us. But he didn't just die; he also lived!

The world Jesus was born into was one of chaos and uncertainty. The Romans had taken Jerusalem in 63 BC, and the people felt their harsh rule. Although the Romans allowed the Jews to keep their customs, the Romans inflicted heavy taxes and new laws with threats of cruelty and oppression. The Romans had newly established an emperor, Caesar Augustus, who began the tradition of emperor worship.[15]

To add to the instability, Herod the Great had been appointed the Jewish ruler over Judea. He was delusional and dangerous. He experienced fits of rage, acted impulsively, and was infamous for murdering anyone who threatened his throne, including members of his own family.[16] While Herod was king, a group of wealthy leaders from the east arrived and explained that they had traveled a great distance because the stars had told them a new king had been born. They had come with gifts with the intent to meet the new king (Matthew 2:1–18). Herod panicked, and in his rage and obsessive desire for power, he ordered the murder of all baby boys under the age of two to try to ensure the death of any child who might usurp his throne.

Into this intense and uncertain political climate, Jesus was born to a young, common girl and her husband. Because of the orders of the Roman emperor, Jesus was born in the small town of Bethlehem, far from his family's home. His mother went into labor just as they arrived in Bethlehem, but they had no place to stay. They were finally given a crude space to sleep, and after his mother gave birth to him, she had to use a trough as a crib (Luke 2:1–7). What a beginning! According to the prophesy laid out about him in Isaiah 53, his life would be filled with pain and suffering.

The authors of the Gospels do not reveal much about the first thirty years of his life but give an account of his last three. In those short three years, the authors document how

Jesus experienced rejection (Matthew 13:57), hunger (Matthew 4:2), physical exhaustion (John 4:6), family conflicts (Mark 3:21), loneliness (Luke 5:16), sorrow (Matthew 26:38), frustration (Mark 9:19), betrayal (Mark 14:44), abandonment by friends (Matthew 26:56), homelessness (Luke 9:58), grief (John 11:35–36), false accusations (Mark 14:57), torture (Mark 15:15), constant harassment from enemies (Mark 3:6), and ultimately murder (Acts 2:23).

If I had been told God was coming to live on this earth for thirty-three years, I would have envisioned him choosing to be born in a safe, God-fearing country, living in a palace, and spending each day teaching and preaching to adoring crowds. But instead, he was born in a humble setting to a poor, young couple, grew up as a carpenter, lived a quiet life, and then chose a path of homelessness and servitude. He *chose* suffering.

The Son of Man's resume of experience in suffering is extensive. His Father and the Spirit partnered with him as he walked this earth, and I can't imagine what it was like for both of them to watch him suffer. Without some sort of purpose, this plan is nothing short of cruel. But he knew what he was doing. He called himself "the son of a human" to show that he was *choosing* a hard life so he could fully understand us.

I sometimes find myself sitting across from my suffering, trying to sort out the dark thoughts it brings and the anxiety that flares up from it, and wondering how my experience could possibly warrant any purpose. I have become an expert in certain areas as far as suffering goes: medical challenges, depression, anxiety, financial hardships, and relationship challenges. If I believed suffering had no point in the grand picture of a God bigger than me, I would be dead.

A huge turning point for me in battling my depression was when I began to realize that the depth of my pain is where my power actually resides. Trust me, as a young girl making plans for college and a future career, the job title "poster child for depression" was not on the list. And if someone had told me I would write a book, the idea of opening with an introduction about a suicide attempt would not have been my dream. But these places of weakness are where I found my power.

I pray to the God who calls himself the "Son of Man." The God who so desperately wanted to know me that he chose to experience my challenges ahead of me so he could relate to me. The Son of Man's pain gives him the power to minister to me. And as he listens to your pain, you become increasingly powerful as you walk through life and experience its hardships. Your suffering can help you to know him better. The more hardship you experience, the more intimately you can *know* Jesus, the more powerful your influence, and the more dangerous you become to Satan. I would argue that Jesus draws especially close to the broken-hearted because he knows what that feels like.

I had a dream years ago that brought this to life. In the dream, I was holding my heart in my hands, and suddenly it slipped and shattered into hundreds of pieces on the floor. I was so shocked. I stood, looking over all the pieces in disbelief. I began to cry. And then, Jesus was there, helping me gather the pieces up, very gently and with reverence. Suddenly, without any words, he showed me how I now had hundreds of pieces to give away. Without my heart being broken, I would have had nothing to offer.

Your suffering is not worthless. Instead of fighting it, press into it, look at it, and begin to find the ways that you can use it to know Jesus and to influence others. Your suffering matters to Jesus, and he handles it with reverence. He *knows* what it feels like because he has been through it. Just like in the story of Zacchaeus you read at the beginning of this chapter, Jesus will find you, come make his home with you, and inspire you.

Bring It to Life

· Look back at Jesus' resume of suffering. Which experiences do you most relate to?

Rejection	Betrayal
Hunger	Abandonment
Physical exhaustion	Homelessness
Family conflict	Grief
Loneliness	False accusation
Sorrow	Physical pain
Frustration	Hatred by others

· Think about your heart. Draw a picture of it, including fracture lines that divide it into pieces. Then label those pieces of your heart with the feelings and experiences that have broken it. For example, I label the pieces of my heart with the words *grief*, *physical pain*, *depression*, *anxiety*, and *exhaustion*.

· Step back and consider how God can use those pieces of your heart. Is there anyone in your life with whom you can relate and understand, whereas others cannot?

Son of Man, the God who desires to know me and experience life as I know it, I pray that during whatever suffering or struggles I am facing or will face, I will lean on the God who truly understands. I pray my heart and mind will continually be open and attentive to how you are using circumstances that feel hopeless and pointless, circumstances that seem only to cause pain. Breathe hope into my hurting, meaning into my suffering, and empower me to use my experiences in a manner that scares Satan and brings glory to your beautifully precious name.

Paraclete

JOHN 14:15–27; GALATIANS 5:13–24; ROMANS 8:1–26

My first day in the psychiatric hospital was disorienting and emotionally confusing. I was assigned to a therapist who felt more like an adversary than a confidant. His job was to evaluate me each day, provide daily therapy sessions, and ultimately decide whether I was healthy enough to go home.

In our first session, he tried to assure me that the events of 9/11, which had recently taken place, had triggered my depression and that it was a dark time in our country, so many people were just like me. It was maddening how little he listened to me. I eventually quit telling him what I was thinking and feeling. With no connection between us, our sessions were pointless. Still, that time was invaluable because it fired up my desire to become a counselor.

Years later, when I was accepted into graduate school to pursue my master's in school counseling, the first course I registered for was called "The Helping Relationship." In it, we learned the importance of skills like empathy, eye contact, active listening, and unconditional positive regard. According to the

American Counseling Association, "Trust is the cornerstone of the counseling relationship."[17] Counseling ethics require therapists to meet the client wherever the client is, provide help that matches their abilities and personal resources, be respectful, not discriminate or intimidate, break down barriers for the client, and bring in resources that the client may need.[18]

Jesus provides the perfect Counselor for us. The word *Paraclete*, which can mean "helper" or "counselor," is often synonymous with the Holy Spirit. The Holy Spirit was Jesus' promised gift before he left. As Jesus' earthly life came closer to the end, he had a sense of urgency about helping his loved ones understand that he would not abandon them. Out of his perfect love, he would send someone to be with them. Jesus provided us with our own personal Counselor, the Holy Spirit. Here are the words Paul uses to describe the qualities that the Holy Spirit brings out in our lives: "Love, joy, peace, forbearance, kindness, goodness, faithfulness, gentleness, and self-control" (Galatians 5:22–23 NIV).

He is the Spirit who lives in you and with you. He loves you. He carries joy and peace. He is patient, kind, good, and faithful to you. He speaks with gentleness and self-control. The Spirit never loses emotional control, and his restraint flows from him and into our lives. His disposition toward you is one of warmth and acceptance. Even by the world's standards, a good counselor and helper builds trust and establishes an alliance with the person whom they're trying to help. The Holy Spirit is the ultimate Counselor.

In the depths of my most depressed days and at the height of my most anxious moments, I have noticed that the tone of my thoughts does not match with how the Spirit communicates. In fact, my thoughts are often downright hateful: *I cannot believe how quickly you're able to mess something up. What kind of Christian are you? Do you honestly think you can do that? What if you screw it up? You should be more like...*

Imagine that a client with clinical depression enters my office and shares his or her fears, doubts, and dark thoughts, to which I reply, "What's wrong with you? You are a Christian! You should be happy and full of joy! Just read your Bible more and pray." Not only would such a reply lack empathy and respect, but it also fails to align with the approach or philosophy of the Spirit. Talking through our thoughts and problems has therapeutic power. As we verbalize what is going on inside our head, we can begin to identify what we truly think and feel and believe.[19] In the presence of a trusted friend or counselor, it is healthy and necessary to speak what is happening in your mind and heart.

What a beautiful opportunity it is to have the most trusted and loving Counselor in the world living inside of us each day! Like a human counselor, the Holy Spirit listens carefully and prays on your behalf, especially when you don't know what to pray. One of the most crucial topics to discuss with him is identifying what emotions you are feeling and what circumstances you might be avoiding in your life. As you pour out your heart to him, listen to the words you use to describe how you *feel*, not simply what you think. If you struggle with identifying an emotion, I recommend going online and printing out a list of emotion words. It might sound simplistic, but it is common to mistakenly cross thoughts with emotions. They are different!

I also recommend talking to your internal Counselor about what you are avoiding. What is the hardest thing to face? The beauty of the Holy Spirit is that he already knows your heart and mind, so you will never shock him, and he can handle anything you want to say. Unlike humans, the Holy Spirit never gets overwhelmed.

Research also shows that talking about relationships is a key part of good mental health.[20] Even if your relationships are solid, talk to the Spirit about the people in your life. As you talk to him, you will explore how the people around you impact you, for better or worse. It is also a good reminder that you can't control anyone, so giving them over to God can be psychologically reassuring.

Scientific evidence also shows that it is healthy to process through your past.[21] You might find it surprising how much of your present behaviors and struggles have connections to things you have gone through in your past. Somehow, God can walk into my memories and lovingly show me new things I never noticed before.

The name *Paraclete* can also be translated as "advocate" or "legal counselor." He is defensive of you because he lives every moment with you and knows your struggles. Imagine going to an attorney for help, and during your consultation, after you have revealed all your deepest and darkest secrets, the attorney says, "Well, you are doomed. You should have known better. Now your only hope is to get out there and try harder. And I am watching your every step. I will remind you of what you need to do, and if you don't, I am going to be very angry." That response would be terrifying and would weigh heavily on the heart and mind. On the contrary, the Holy Spirit knows what you are up against, and his role is to remind you of things you have learned in the Bible and to help you apply them. And when you fail (because you will), he is ready to pick you up, carry you before the Father, and speak encouragement over you, alleviating the weight of your burdens.

If harsh thoughts cross your mind, they are not from the Holy Spirit and do not align with his approach to you. He might show you difficult things and push you toward change, but he does so with respect, kindness, and gentleness. Nothing in the Bible supports the idea that life is easy, so he expects that you will struggle and you will fail, and he stands ready to pick you up.

Often those of us with depression have harsh thoughts. There is so much freedom when we realize that our God *knows* we will struggle. He knows we need a good Counselor and Advocate with us at all times, so be aware that those harshly toned thoughts are not from him.

Bring It Home

- What emotions and thoughts do you have about yourself? Write them down.

- What is the tone of those thoughts? Does it align with the person of the Holy Spirit? Remember, he might give you reminders or push you toward change, but his tone is not accusing or unkind.

- In contrast, what would a loving counselor and friend say to you? What thoughts and emotions does God have about you?

- Look for words that tend to be linked to harsh thoughts. Words like *always* and *never* and *should have*.

Jesus, the One who gifted me with the Counselor and Advocate I so desperately need, I pray my heart will find comfort and rest in the arms of the One who knows me and truly understands me. I pray for my thoughts to be transformed into the gentle and kind and patient tone you take with me. I pray I will have the ability to picture the depth of the love the Holy Spirit feels on my behalf and to see his commitment to bringing me hope and peace and rest.

DAY 5

Almighty God

JOB 38–42:6; PSALM 113:1–6

When I was younger, I wasn't sure if I wanted to have kids, but once I fell in love with the idea, I wanted to have a lot of kids. I envisioned having a home bustling with energy, lots of love, and connectedness.

Tim and I were very excited when we found out I was pregnant, and the first four months went well. But around the fifth month, I began to have contractions and ended up on bedrest for the remainder of my pregnancy. The doctors were successful in holding off my labor, and Carter Pace was born on Easter morning, healthy and doing well. However, I was not doing well, and soon my situation turned critical. My lungs were full of fluid, my kidneys became badly infected, and I had a pulmonary embolism. I needed so many different types of medications that both of my arms had IVs. The road to recovery was slow and painful.

My doctor met with me and discussed the dangers of another pregnancy, and Tim and I prayed earnestly for wisdom. After months of debating and grieving, I got a hysterectomy, and

37

we worked to accept that we would not have any more biological children. Strike one.

We decided to go for an international adoption, and we reasoned that this was why God had closed my ability to carry more children. We spent a few years saving up the money to start the process, went to the first meeting at Children's Home Society in Minneapolis, and decided on the program through Ethiopia. We were excited and energized!

Then Tim lost his job suddenly. I couldn't support our family solely on my income, and we needed the adoption fund to survive. Each month, we bit into the adoption fund, and the dream and energy we were carrying slowly died. Strike two.

Seven years later, we decided to try adopting again. My parents offered to help financially. After carefully reviewing different agencies and programs, we chose one through Uganda that seemed to be the right fit. We did the paperwork and watched the online classes. As I was working on scheduling our home study, I received the news that my mom had come down with a serious illness. After prayer, we realized we had to move from our home in North Carolina to Minnesota to help her. Since our adoption agency was based in North Carolina, a move out of state would make things tricky. We still hoped to make it work, but after moving across the country, we had to obtain new jobs, which led to financial insecurities. Still, we fought on. And then Uganda closed its borders and was no longer allowing international adoptions. Strike three.

I had bouts of anger and frustration and grief. I shared my pain and hurt with others. Unfortunately, many told me things that just made the situation harder. Things like, "Well, at least you have Carter," or "It's just not meant to be."

I had spent my college years planning my life: get married, have multiple kids, become a pastor's wife. When I was at work and someone complained about how busy they were with so many kids, I ached internally. When Facebook friends posted loving pictures of their large families, I grieved.

I worked as a school counselor and sometimes had to call social services on abusive home situations. And as I filed the report, often working to save multiple children in a family, my heart was heavy. My conversations with God became pointed. I prayed, *Why? Why can't we have more children? We are good parents. Look at those people; they are not good parents, and you gave them more kids than you gave us. Why would you withhold something from me that you say in your Word is good? I mean, didn't you call us to have children?*

My anger subsided for a while. I would return to the rhythm of life, and then something would ignite all those terrible feelings and grief, and my prayers returned to angry accusations.

The first time I read God's speech in Job, it took me aback. His tone is distinctly assertive, and instead of scaring me, it drew me in. It was the realization that he is so big, so powerful, and so beyond me that my small mind questioning his cosmic mind is pure foolishness. I began to realize that my life was like a book, and I assumed I was the author. Instead, I am the main character, and I am reading it one page at a time. Each day is one page in this ever-unraveling novel that God has already foreseen. His plot is so much thicker and more complicated than one I would have chosen!

I had a dream one night that I was standing at a podium in front of a huge leather-bound book that waited for me to open it. I opened it. And there on gold pages were all kinds of lines and charts and markings. I realized it was a book of all the possibilities in the universe of my life and all the various outcomes. It was one enormous equation—every inch of my life analyzed and drawn out. It was so incredibly complicated that it felt as if I were looking at another language. And although the book had been quite large upon its discovery, I soon realized that it appeared to be endless.

Suddenly, God stood beside me, not saying a word, just watching me. As I turned each page, I became increasingly overwhelmed. The chart I had drawn for my life had only one line with dates and expectations. God's version was vastly more complex.

In regard to the adoption process, I see things now that I didn't then. There are so many reasons why it was better that we didn't get to adopt when I wanted to. Our adoption fund ran out quickly. We lost everything and had to move to North Carolina to survive on what little we had left. We could barely make ends meet with one child. Upon moving to North Carolina, we struggled to find jobs, so we both ended up going back to graduate school. Grad school meant long nights of papers and exam prep. Thankfully, Carter was old enough to also be in school, so often we would all study together.

Although moving to Minnesota disrupted our second adoption attempt, it gave me a chance to pursue starting my own practice, which led to speaking engagements, which brought a publisher, who proposed a book. So, had I adopted a child when I wanted to, this book and our connection to each other never would have existed.

Trust him. He loves you. He paid a dear price to be close to you. He has put the ultimate amount of effort and thought into your story. More than you will ever know.

Bring It to Life

- In your journal, write out what you feel have been turning points in your life. What do you notice?

- What are your impressions of God's speech at the end of Job? Look carefully through his resume and choose which claim stands out to you the most. For me, the "store houses of snow" in Job 38:22 (NIV) has always stood out, maybe because I live in Minnesota. So when we have a huge snowstorm, I am reminded of God's greatness. Choose which visual he uses that stands out to you, and when you see it in your world, let it remind you of who he is.

- Write out the vision you have for your life and talk to the almighty God about it. Speak openly with him about your grief over broken dreams and precious losses.

Almighty God, the One who existed before time began, who has infinite knowledge, understanding, wisdom, and love, I pray to you. As I walk through each page of my life, I pray I will find confidence that you have seen my path. You know what is best for me since you have intimate knowledge of all the corners of my life, things I can't see and things I may never know. I pray to find the supernatural strength to trust you. You are a loving God, the Almighty, who knows all things, to whom I can entrust my story.

Redeemer

EXODUS 12:1–14, 29–42;
ISAIAH 43:1–5; 1 JOHN 1:9

Redeem (verb): to buy back or win back; to free from what distresses or harms: such as to free from captivity by payment of a ransom; to extricate from or help overcome something detrimental; to release blame or debt; to free from the consequence of sin; to change for the better.[22]

Tim used to participate in prison ministry at a maximum-security prison in South Carolina. He told me how vexing it was to sit with a number of hardened men and listen to them wistfully discuss how much they missed and loved their children. It seemed like such an odd paradox. Pharaoh was also a very hardened man. He watched his subjects and his own family suffer immensely under the punishment of God, but in his pride and hatred, he would not bow to God's demand to free the Israelites from their slavery. With each plague, his resolve intensified. God knew there was one thing he could take away that would break even the hardest of men. There was one life in Egypt that held the key to the freedom of his people.

In his final plague, God took the life of all the first-born sons in Egypt, which included Pharaoh's son. The Egyptians had been murdering the sons of the Israelites, so this plague was extremely personal. The death of that one child broke Pharaoh's resolve. In his grief, Pharaoh consented to let the Israelites go.

It is incredible to think that centuries later, the Father would turn that curse on himself and request that his only Son die on behalf of you and me. If a hardened and evil man like Pharaoh can be broken by the death of a son, how much more will the heart of a loving and compassionate Father break!

The majority of the passages in the Old Testament that name God as the "Redeemer" reference the exodus story. It was a foreshadowing of what the actual redemption would look like. The determination to rescue you was powered by the overwhelming love that the Father, the Son, and the Holy Spirit have for you.

To make it more personal, imagine that you have been convicted of a heinous crime; your guilt is undeniable. Because of the severity of your offense, you know you will be receiving the death penalty. As you rise before the judge, you explain your remorse, your sorrow, your regrets. He gently tells you that he knew long before you were born that this day was coming. Before you even committed your crimes, he and his son and your attorney had all met and developed a plan. His only son had agreed to receive the torture and death penalty on your behalf. The judge, his son, and your attorney all love you and together were determined to save you. They knew you would need help as you leave to start your new life, so your attorney would be going with you. The judge and his son would also be with you, always available to talk with you.

The judge gives you his book, which contains all you need to know as you start your new life. And you are told to go in peace, start fresh, and not to be afraid. The death penalty the judge's son paid has more than fulfilled your crimes. It has covered you not only for your past but also for your future. *Go in peace.*

Imagine you and your attorney leaving the courtroom, but as you get home, you begin cutting out any newspaper clippings or articles about your past crimes so you can relive it as punishment to yourself. You mentally and emotionally revisit your failings, turning them over and over in your mind. You tell yourself you do not deserve to live in peace. Can you relate?

I have suffered from watching what I call my "bad movies." These are the reruns of my worst moments: the times when I hurt others, made terrible choices that resulted in horrible consequences, and failed to do the right thing. Even after repenting, turning to a new path, and living a new life, I often find those bad movies haunting me, especially when I am tired or discouraged.

Reliving our past makes flourishing in the present impossible. The truth is, the more horrible your past, the more incredibly powerful Christ's sacrifice. To go back to our example, perhaps taking the punishment for someone speeding would seem a lot less impressive than taking the punishment for a murderer. The darker your past, the more incredible the power of his sacrifice. Letting go of your past failings is essential to breaking free from depression. You may still be struggling with consequences of your past choices, but that is vastly different from allowing your past to steal your emotional and mental freedom.

Another visual God provides for this concept is being washed clean. No matter how hard I try, I will eventually need another shower, but the water and soap always seem to work.

(Sometimes it takes more soap than other days!) Psalm 51 is a great example of the concept of being cleansed. It was written by King David, who had an affair and then murdered his friend, the woman's husband. Through the prophet Nathan, David was confronted with his sin and wrote Psalm 51 in response as he repented of his crimes. What's beautiful is that his prayer not only discusses getting cleansed but also turning his guilt and pain into "joy and gladness" (Psalm 51:8 NIV). The Redeemer declared you innocent. He cleanses you on a daily, hourly, minute-by-minute basis. He delights in doing it, and it was hard-earned.

To return to the freedom of the Israelites, you will notice the houses with lamb's blood, which represented the future sacrifice of the Redeemer, Jesus, were safe. After the Israelites were set free, they traveled to the Red Sea and were horrified to discover that Pharaoh's grief had turned to anger, and he pursued them with his army. The Israelites found themselves trapped by the Red Sea. In their terror, they assumed the Pharaoh would get his final revenge for the death of his son by killing them all. However, Pharaoh, his army, and the Israelites all underestimated the power and meticulous planning of the Redeemer.

God parted the sea, which created a pathway for his peoples' escape. While the Israelites crossed the sea on dry ground, God held the Egyptian army back so they could not attack. And when the Egyptians attempted to pursue the Israelites through the sea, God waited until they made it halfway, then he disassembled their chariots and created chaos. God let the water go back into its place, thus destroying Pharaoh's entire army.

What an incredible experience! What a display of God's passion for freedom! However, life was still not easy for the Israelites. For the next forty years, God had them wander in the desert, leading them one step at a time. Although life in the desert was difficult, the Israelites were no longer slaves; they were free.

You are no longer a slave to your past. Jesus bought your freedom with his blood. You now walk in emotional and mental freedom, despite how hard this life can be. Don't let your past sins convince you that you are still in slavery and not free. The Redeemer said it best: "It is finished" (John 19:30 NIV).

Bring It Home

· What bad movies replay in your head?

· Read Luke 7:36–50.

· Compare and contrast Simon with the woman. What do you notice?

· Write out what Jesus says to her in Luke 7:50 and meditate on that; what are the implications of that statement for your life?

My Redeemer, you are the One who paid for my freedom, so my past does not define my present or my future. I pray for freedom from the past. Lord, God, Redeemer, please break any chains of slavery that are holding me back from the freedom you paid so dearly for. I beg you to provide healing, comfort, and help as I try to "go in peace." Each time one of those bad movies appears, I pray you will take me back to the heavenly courtroom, where you and your Father and the Spirit all agreed, "It is finished!"

Vine

JOHN 15:1-12; GALATIANS 5:22–23;
2 CORINTHIANS 5:14–21

My husband and I love watching the show *Dateline*. The plot is essentially always the same: follow the journey of a criminal and see him or her brought to justice. Sometimes Tim and I read or hear about a criminal act in the news, and we look at each other and say, "That sounds like a future *Dateline* episode!"

Let's examine some familiar characters who deserve their own *Dateline* episodes. If they were alive today, these would be their charges:

- Moses: second-degree murder (Exodus 2:11–12)

- Rahab: prostitution (Joshua 2)

- David: first-degree murder of a close and loyal friend (2 Samuel 11)

- Abraham: perjury (Genesis 12:10–20)

- Noah: drunken and disorderly conduct (Genesis 9:20–29)

- Rebekah and Jacob: fraud (Genesis 27)

- Paul (whose name was Saul before he became a follower of Jesus): first-degree murder in numerous counts; conspiracy to commit murder (Acts 7:54–8:3)

This is the list of their criminal charges, but they also committed other offenses that fell short of crimes. However, some of these men and women are champions of our faith, and we look to them for inspiration and guidance. If they were living today, we would be visiting many of them in prison. How can that be possible?

One conclusion is that they did not become leaders of our faith based on their impeccably pure reputations. The other logical conclusion is that their crimes did not destroy their hopes of living an inspirational life. Along with their criminal records, they share other things in common: They had a relationship with God; they trusted him and were convinced that he cared about them. And each of them loved and followed God in return.

I am grateful that the women and men who provided such foundational leadership for our faith had such deep failings. I have had so many Christians come to my office in a dark depression, and the first thing they say to me is, "I am not a good Christian." As the discussion continues, I often see that their way of thinking has convinced them that they *are* their sin.

I will be the first to admit that I am not a "good Christian." I could choose any number of my personal failings as an example for you. One of the most trying for me has been my battle with an addiction to prescription drugs and over-the-counter medications as an undergraduate at a Christian university. I spent several years finding ways to transfer my dependence on medications to dependence on God. The transformation did not come overnight. I struggled with shame over my battle. I heard people say that they could never imagine the type of person who ends up addicted to drugs. I cringed inside and prayed that my secret would remain just that: a secret.

I used to call myself a drug abuser. Then I realized that I, Jenita Pace, am not a prescription drug abuser; I am someone who struggles with an addiction to prescription drugs. This epiphany was incredibly liberating. A simple change in my terminology took root in my fight against addiction, and I have found freedom from that part of my life. For a long time, I tucked that piece of my story away, hoping it would remain a secret. I feared my addiction somehow disqualified me from being used powerfully by Jesus.

Depression thrives on stealing your identity and convincing you that your actions define who you are. Your actions do not determine your identity; your identity is tied directly to Jesus, the Vine. He is the One who provides the nutrients you need to grow, nutrients you cannot obtain on your own. Paul's conclusion is that as you stay connected and walk with the Spirit, the growth you want to experience begins naturally (Galatians 5:22–23). I am not suggesting that this freedom gives us license to sin as we please. I developed skills to overcome my addiction, and it required a significant amount of work. It has been liberating to experience the transformation, and I'm grateful for it.

When we talk about David, we do not refer to him as "David, the murderer." We do not refer to Noah as "Noah, the alcoholic" or "Paul, the serial killer." God chose not to cover up their sins but to expose them to all humanity so that we would marvel at his ability to turn failure into success. Depression will try to convince you that because of your current failings, you are hopeless, like a fruit tree trying to grow without roots.

Jesus calls himself a vine and describes each of us as branches attached to him. The health of the vine determines the health of the fruit on those branches. My prayer is that you see yourself as fruit clinging to the Vine, who provides nutrients for your growth. You can find those nutrients in Jesus' words through his book, the Bible. Thank goodness our Vine is healthy, strong, loving, kind, generous, and compassionate!

Added to the power of knowing you are not your sin is the feeling of freedom to enjoy authentic relationships with others. I wonder what it would be like if David visited our church. Would he find confidence in openly shaking hands and meeting new people, or would it haunt him that everyone in the sanctuary knew all the lurid details of his affair and murder charges, not to mention a host of other failings he had as a parent? Would he be sitting in the pew wishing he could bolt?

My hope is that he would see the power his story has had for inspiring many of us who have lived less than perfect lives. The Lord is searching for those who are spiritually starving so he can fill them up and transform them. This immediate transformation is so radical that the Bible describes us as a "new creation," and that status does not change (2 Corinthians 5:17 NIV).

I know it is likely that at some point, you will be watching a trial on your TV. Maybe it will be on a documentary like *Dateline*. Perhaps you will see a trial play out on the evening news, in a movie, or on a crime show drama that you enjoy watching. As the villain in the story faces sentencing, picture Jesus standing up from the audience, pointing to the criminal being sentenced, and in front of everyone present, he exclaims, "I cannot wait to have more time with *you! You* are exactly the kind of person I am looking for!" You are not your sin!

Bring It to Life

· Read Galatians 2:17–21. Write out what this passage means for you. Imagine Christ taking a piece of wood and nailing your sin titles to it—and then leaving it there. Christ didn't stay on the cross; he came down from it and rose from the dead. He left both his punishment and your sin titles on the cross.

· Each time you see a cross, picture your sin title nailed to it and having it die with Christ. If you really struggle with this concept, you might want to get a piece of wood and some nails. Write the titles you have given yourself based on your sins and nail them to the board. The energy Christ took in destroying your sin titles cannot be overstated.

· When you are enjoying eating fruit, use that moment to meditate on the incredible beauty he brings out in you. Stay connected to him through continuing to read his book, the Bible.

Jesus, the Vine who provides the nutrients for our transformation, I pray you will help each of us to fully recognize the power you have to destroy any sin titles in our lives. I pray that I will actually experience the freedom of knowing that my name is not attached to my sin. Instead, you have broken the chains of any failings and made them flawless before you. I pray for freedom from any sins I am combating; I pray that I will continually draw from the nutrients that come from your Word and that I will continue to experience transformation in you.

DAY 8

Doctor

MARK 2:13–17; PROVERBS 13:12

Anyone who has been around our family knows we go to the hospital a lot. For some reason, my husband is either injured or sick, just recovered from being injured or sick, or is about to get injured or sick. The joke with our family and closest friends is that everyone gets a turn taking Tim to the emergency room.

There have been times when his injuries were produced from his own misjudgments: like the time he cut his thumb showing me the "right way" to slice a bagel in half or the motorcycle accident when he miscalculated a turn and slid off the road. There have been times when he was injured because of someone else's mistake, like his ambulance ride to the hospital after a woman ran a stoplight and collided with Tim's car or the time when a kid accidentally kicked him in the head at a youth retreat. And then there were the injuries and sicknesses that we cannot attribute to anyone, like the time he had severe kidney stones or the visit to the hospital for a random seizure. And somehow, amidst all of it, he keeps a positive attitude. The man is amazing!

Each time we have visited an emergency room, we encounter a physician who usually asks a lot of questions, sets up medical tests, plans on how to meet Tim's needs, and sends us home with instructions for continued care. We haven't encountered a doctor who would listen to what happened and respond with, "I don't know. I mean, he's injured because he was negligent. I only treat those who are not responsible for their own injuries." Or imagine if the doctor said, "So, your injuries are due to a car accident that was not your fault? I really need the driver of the other car, the woman who ran the stoplight, here. She needs to be the one to do the work since this is technically her fault."

I think about the times in my life when my emotional and mental injuries are my own doing. Something inside tells me that because of my own negligence, I have no right to bring it to Jesus. I hurt myself, so I should fix it. Or in times when others have injured me, I want the guilty party to take responsibility and heal me.

Jesus has a particular heart for the wounded. As the Doctor for our spirits, he knows our injuries, and regardless of the cause, he wants us to call on him to provide care. Much like a physician, he wants to dialogue with you, to listen to your complaints, and to provide resources to bring healing. Healing involves accepting his help and following his guidance.

Dealing with the sickness of depression is a lot of work. I have had clients tell me their goal is to conquer their battle with depression and anxiety. I have had people explain in desperation that they feel like failures because, although they feel better, somehow the depression and anxiety return. They want it just to end, to move on, and to no longer face off with their old and familiar internal enemies.

I have found freedom in accepting that I will always battle with depression and anxiety. It may sound backwards, but I found hope and relief when I suddenly realized that yes, I would likely battle depression and anxiety for the rest of my life, and because of that, it would force me to continually visit Jesus, my Doctor, every day. Battling depression and anxiety gives me the gift of recognizing my need for Jesus. I am so fragile; I cannot survive without having direct consultations with my Doctor every day. I am so spiritually sick that I cannot chance missing time with him. I am so weak that I cannot go a day without reading his words and applying them to my life.

In the story recorded in Mark 2, the "sinners" were those who were aware that they needed help, the ones who recognized their need for a doctor. They invited Jesus to dinner, desiring time with him, and Mark records that many of them believed him. The religious leaders of the day, the Pharisees, had made religion so burdensome that the crowd of social rejects included people like prostitutes, criminals, and social outcasts, as well as people who couldn't keep up with the religious rules and expectations.[23] These were people who were aware of their need for help. However, the religious leaders did not see a need for Jesus because, in their assessment, they did not require any assistance. They had become so confident in their self-sufficiency that it blocked their ability to see the depth of their sinful nature. It is a strange blessing to carry something that continually reminds us of our greatest need.

Just like physical injuries, our heart injuries manifest themselves in symptoms that signal to us that we need help. For me, when my anxiety has become too powerful, I will have panic attacks that make me stutter, and I become unable to speak. My mind will get stuck in a loop, and I find it hard not to repeat myself. I was looking for a way to stop my panic attacks, believing that these attacks were the problem. I finally realized that my body was talking to me. It was telling me that I had pushed my body and mind and spirit too hard and needed to stop. With my depression, when it is gaining strength, I become reclusive, sleep too much, and get overcome with feelings of worthlessness and shame.

My symptoms tell me something: I need more time with my heavenly Doctor. I need to take in his words, the medication that directly speaks to my pain. I need time with other believers to help me understand the truth in his words. Regardless of why I am sick, Jesus wants to be the One to offer the care. He will use your body to give you signals about what you need and provide practical resources around you.

I have had well-meaning clients who tell me they just want to depend on the Bible for getting well, which I understand is coming from a desire to depend on Jesus alone. I appreciate that desire! However, there are so many tools and resources available that I think are direct gifts from our great Doctor. I always encourage my clients to pursue all avenues of getting healthy, which sometimes include medications as well as making sure to get enough sleep, getting exercise, and eating well. Our souls reside in our earthly bodies, and we need to care for the whole being. But those things alone won't address your deepest need: your soul's healing.

The medical code of ethics states, "The relationship between a patient and a physician is based on trust, which gives rise to a physician's ethical responsibility to place patients' welfare above the physician's own interest or obligations to others."[24] Oh, thank goodness Jesus is the Physician who gave up his own life to greet us when we come injured into his presence.

Bring It to Life

· Create three columns in your journal: Emotional, Mental, and Physical.

· In each column, what are you doing currently to keep your emotions, mind, and body healthy? In what areas do you specifically need help? Here are some areas to consider in each of the three dimensions:

Emotional	Mental	Physical
Recognize what you feel and how to express it in a healthy way; talk to trusted loved ones; see a therapist	Monitor thoughts and their tones, particularly avoiding shame; see a therapist	Maintain a sleep schedule, exercise, avoid misusing substances, take medications if needed, consume a nutritious diet

Our divine Doctor, the One who runs to the sick and is ready and willing to help, who desires to bring healing. I pray right now that I will see what my heart needs. I pray I will feel no shame or fear in bringing to you my brokenness, regardless of whether it is because of my own bad choices, someone else's bad choices, or simply the pain of life. May I enter your presence knowing you are eager to offer your help. Oh great Doctor, I pray the medication of your words will provide the soothing relief I am so desperate for. I thank you for showing me how sick I am so I can fully understand how much I need you.

Day 9

Friend

JOHN 15:9–17; MARK 2:1–12; ROMANS 5:6–9

A wealth of research has shown that humans are not meant to live in isolation. Social isolation can increase levels of stress hormones, which can disrupt sleep and result in a compromised immune system. It is not uncommon for people who have been in an extreme form of isolation to begin, over time, to halluci-nate, creating imaginary friends to have a connection to. Our brain literally cannot handle being alone.[25]

It is important to have people in our lives who genuinely love and care about us. Keep in mind that not even God is alone; he exists in three persons. He created us with a need for loving human connections that is imperative to our mental health. A standard question I always ask my clients is, "Who is supporting you during this time?"

When my depression first hit, I demanded that my husband keep my challenge a secret. I was afraid that if people found out I was struggling, especially fellow Christians, that I would be judged and rejected. In that process, I also isolated my husband, who needed the support of others as much as I did. After my hospitalization, there was no way to hide the depths of my mental darkness, and my experience with our pastor and the elders at our church proved that, yes, there was validity to my fear that some Christians would misunderstand and mishandle my pain. But there were also Christians who reached out their hands and allowed us to fall into their arms.

Steve and Pat Bradley boldly approached us and advocated for their right to help us. My mom worked to find a therapy program, which ended up being a turning point in my journey. Although Tim did not understand my depression, he was dedicated to learning as much about it as he could. All four of them played a vital role in my survival. But Tim later told me how difficult it was to be alone and not able to open up to his friends about our struggles during my depression. Looking back, I see that I hindered my own growth by not allowing Tim to reach out for support from those he trusted and loved. It was short-sighted of me, and I was not considering his needs. We could have obtained resources immediately had I been open to sharing our situation with more people.

Now, when we face a challenge, I tend to reach out to people more quickly and to seek out counsel from others who have been through similar situations. It is like when you stop and ask a local for directions when lost; turning to others to get help navigating new terrain can save a lot of time and preserve precious energy. And when you allow people to really *know* you, it may be easier to access help when trouble hits. A good, trusted friend can sometimes identify what you need before you or your family can recognize it.

The story of the paralytic in Mark 2 is a powerful example of four people determined to find help for their friend. Jesus was teaching in Peter's house. The roof above him would likely have been made of mud-plastered branches spread over rafters. The four friends would literally have dug through the roof to lower their friend in front of Jesus.[26] What an incredible act of love! What an incredible determination of faith! They just knew that if they could bring their friend before a loving God, he would have a chance for true healing. I assume they didn't know Jesus would address both his spiritual and physical needs.

It is interesting that the story in the Greek language doesn't use the word *friends* to describe these four people. The word is simply "four people."[27] The assumption is that they had some sort of intimate connection to him because why else would anyone put that kind of effort into saving someone? The concept of "friendship" in the Bible is a word that implies experience and action.

Jesus calls himself your friend. He is the "friend of sinners" (Matthew 11:19), which implies the obviously broken and distressed. He developed a reputation for spending time with people who were known to be the most spiritually lost in society. He is that trusted friend who knows what you need before you do. And the people who lowered their friend before Jesus trusted that Jesus would be the ultimate friend and not let them down. Jesus' definition of his friendship to you supersedes the common expectations of society. He is willing to make the ultimate sacrifice in giving his life up for his friends (John 15:13).

Jesus openly states that he loves us. According to the Bible's definition of love, Jesus is patient, kind, not self-seeking, not jealous, not boastful, not prideful, not dishonest, not easily angered, does not keep a record of your wrongs, does not delight in evil, rejoices in truth, always protects, always trusts, always hopes, and always perseveres (see 1 Corinthians 13:4–7). This is the friend we so desperately need!

It is important that you have people who lower you before Jesus. I realize that means being authentic and seeking out help.

I am not going to give you false assurances; there is a real risk that you might be criticized and blamed for your own depression. You might have well-meaning people give you all kinds of terrible advice and judge you. However, you are not meant to do this alone. The people who are your best allies will be attentive to your needs, remind you that Jesus is your friend, and lower you before him continually. Good friends don't just offer their support and kindness, but they also tell us the tough things we don't want to hear. We need loving accountability.

On the other end of the spectrum is surrounding yourself with many people, none of whom know you well. The paralytic had four people who knew him well enough to know what his needs were and who knew he wanted to see Jesus. I have met clients who tell me how lonely they are despite having thousands of friends on social media and being surrounded by people constantly. Jesus set an example of companionship by choosing twelve men—twelve individuals with whom he would have a focused relationship. We know he traveled with more people than just those twelve, but he invested heavily in those few relationships.

Be intentional about choosing those with whom you spend time. Make sure you are not avoiding authentic relationships by filling your time with multiple surface relationships. Do not isolate yourself. Draw near to your friend, Jesus. And seek out the friendship and connections of those who can help. If you already have those people in your life, get authentic with them and allow them to lower you before Jesus.

· Whom do you have in your life who can lower you before Jesus? Are you allowing them to do that for you? If not, what is holding you back?

· If you have people in your life who are trying to help but are doing more harm than good, then make a list of what you need. Don't assume your friends and loved ones know what you need. Allow your loved ones to secure their own support system so they can help you.

· Look within and beyond your social circle to find someone whom you can help lower before Jesus. It is incredibly rewarding. Whenever I try to stop my good friend Sarita from helping me, she playfully says, "Jenita, don't steal my blessing!"

Keep in mind that your friends will make mistakes sometimes. They might say or do something unhelpful. Give them grace as they figure out how to help. If you don't have people supporting you, I recommend reaching out to local churches with counseling ministries. Pursue therapy. Even if your initial appointment with a therapist is not a positive experience (like mine!), do not give up. Keep searching for the right person.

Jesus, the friend of the broken-hearted, I pray that you will provide friends, good friends, who will lower me before you. I pray for a counselor who will do the same. I ask you, Jesus, to bring me confidence to reach out for help and not to assume I can do this alone. You don't even do life alone! Jesus, provide wisdom and insight to the people trying to help, that they might be transformed in the process of lowering me before you.

Alpha and Omega

REVELATION 1:4–8; 21:3–6; ECCLESIASTES 3:1–11

Guillain-Barré syndrome is a rare autoimmune condition in which a person's immune system turns on their nervous system and begins attacking it viciously. Before February 2016, I had never even heard of it, let alone met anyone with it. But that winter, I became very familiar with it.

I was living in North Carolina at the time and received a call from my dad in Minnesota telling me that my mom was suddenly unable to walk. He had taken her into the hospital, and she was not coming home with him. Something was very wrong. Soon after, he sent me a picture of the white board in her hospital room with the diagnosis written on it in red letters: "Guillain-Barré syndrome."

Fast forward a week, and I was sitting in an ICU room in Minneapolis. Guillain-Barré, as it happens, is a very powerful force. Within days, my mom had lost all ability to move, except to shake her head. She had even lost the ability to close her eyes. Every time she wanted to sleep, we would tape them shut for her.

The most agonizing part of the journey was her inability to communicate. She couldn't talk or gesture or point, but she was fully alive mentally, trapped in her body. Because of her limitations, we scheduled someone to sit with her at the hospital around the clock. I usually took daytime shifts, which consisted of watching her constantly, trying to sort out what she wanted or needed.

It was a strange experience—missing someone you spent hours with each day. As I sat with her, sometimes I listened to old voicemails she had left me, just to hear her voice. We put up family pictures in her hospital room, which we were told would offer her encouragement. I found that those pictures did more for me than for her. I was clinging to any image or sound that would remind me of her.

There is no cure for Guillain-Barré, but there are treatments to try to stop the immune system from attacking the nervous system. Each treatment seemed to inch us in the right direction, but it was slow going and full of heartbreak.

One day, I remember Mom was trying to communicate with me, to tell me something that she wanted. After some confusing head shaking and guessing, I realized she was asking for a clock and a calendar. There is something comforting about time. In the panic of meeting her needs, it did not occur to me that without a clock and a calendar, she had no way of interpreting what was going to happen and when. The psychological impact that would have had not dawned on me. We bought a clock and placed it close to her, and my aunt put together a large calendar to hang on her wall.

God is outside of time. But what is beautiful is that he created time and put himself in it for us. The name Alpha and Omega (the first and last letters of the Greek alphabet) signify that he is at the beginning and all the way to the end. Without his decision to create time and give us the ability to mark progress in our life, there would be no beginning and no end. It is in his grace and his wisdom that he understands we need some way to see life progress—some way to mark out our inching toward the end.

Not only was the designation of time important for my mom, but it was for me, as well. Slowly, painfully, she began to show progress. It started with slight movement of her right thumb. As her immune system stopped its attack and her nerves worked to heal, she gradually got her body back, one inch at a time. I remember the first day she was able to speak again. It was such a lovely moment! I remember the day she came home and the first time she was able to practice walking in physical therapy. Jesus was absolutely present in every moment of that horrific journey.

The book of Ecclesiastes reminds us that things change in time. There are moments that are beautiful, marked as a time of celebration. And there are times when life is excruciating and slow. Regardless of where you are, there is hope in knowing that God is in every minute of your life. And he purposely has created a system whereby you can know that you are moving ahead in time. He has already lived in your future, he knows your past intimately, and he asks you to stay with him in the present. I have had times in my life when I have focused too much on the past. Sometimes I replay poor choices I have made, regret opportunities I have missed out on, or long for times in my life that seemed so much better than the present.

When my focus gets too narrowed in on the past, I notice that it feeds my depression. I can't do anything to change or relive what has already been. I also noticed that sometimes I get too focused on the future, wishing certain things would come true, working to try to bring a dream to life, or worrying about what might happen. When my focus gets too narrowed on the future, my anxiety tends to grow out of control.

The hardest moments during my story have been when the suffering does not have an obvious end in sight. During the challenges I face, it is frustrating that I can't look at a calendar and see the end date. However, it is important to keep grounded in the present day while also finding hope that God promises there will be an end to our suffering. The end might not come for a long time, but the suffering will end someday. Time is moving you to that end. God is using this name to comfort you and guide you. He has been through the story of the world, from the beginning to the end. In the same way, he has been in *your* story from the beginning to the end. He wants you to stay with him in the moment in time you are in right now.

I love how Ecclesiastes 3 indicates that eternity is in all our hearts. We all long to be at a resting place, where we no longer need time to push us forward. But until we get there, marvel at how God continues to give us the ability to live in increments of time. And stay with him in whatever part of the calendar he currently has you in.

· Where does your mind currently reside most often? In the past, present, or future? Why?

· When you see a clock or a calendar, be reminded of the gift God gave by creating a way for you to measure time. Be aware that he is always moving you forward.

· The term *mindfulness* refers to ways to keep centered on the present when your mind wants to go to the past or to the future in ways that cause distress. To stay in the present, it sometimes helps to do things that keep your attention in the here and now, techniques called grounding. *Grounding* refers to things you can physically do to keep your mind in the present.

· You can find a list of suggestions online for grounding. I hold an ice pack in my hand and focus on the sensation of the cold. Concentrating on the temperature brings my mind to attention and focuses it when I am feeling anxious and overwhelmed.

Our dear Alpha and Omega, the God who is present at the very beginning of the story and stays true and steady to the end, I pray that you will bring your healing, guidance, and wisdom. I pray, Alpha and Omega, that in whatever situation is happening around me or in me, whatever is on my heart and in my mind, your eternal presence will always bring comfort and hope and peace. You know my past, are in my present, and have already walked my future. Bring your supernatural peace and rest.

Carpenter and Cornerstone

MARK 6:2–3; ISAIAH 53:1–3;
PHILIPPIANS 2:5–8; 1 PETER 2:4–8

God's design is beyond me. If God had consulted me on what type of employment he should take while living on this planet, I would have suggested a teacher, religious leader, or government official. However, God chose to become a carpenter.

The job of a carpenter in the ancient world was tough both physically and mentally. It required a lot of strength, calculated skills, and practice. Carpenters tended to fall into two categories: some were hired to construct buildings and houses while others focused on making household items, like furniture. The tools were crude, and the work was not glamorous or celebrated. Families tended to work together, so it is likely that Jesus' father and brothers were his co-workers.[28] Imagine Jesus spending his years sawing, sanding, measuring, nailing, and building.

Jesus spent more time in the trade industry than in public ministry. When Jesus finally came forward and made his claim that he was the Messiah, it was hard for his family, friends, and neighbors to believe him because he was so normal and unimpressive. God had chosen to live a seemingly average life. And to add to his normalcy, even his name was nothing spectacular. The name *Jesus* was very common at that time. Jesus likely grew up with friends and relatives who shared his first name. The name *Jesus* means "the Lord saves," which is the equivalent of embodying salvation, so it was fitting.[29] Many parents probably named their sons "Jesus" to indicate their hopes and dreams about the coming savior. And so, he was extremely normal: Jesus the carpenter.

I wonder what it was like for him to go to the synagogue and listen to the priests and religious leaders teach. For thirty years, he entered the synagogue, sat with the people, and listened to others interpret his words, Sabbath after Sabbath. The God of the universe chose to sit, listen, and wait for his Father to tell him when it was time for him to become the teacher. Have you experienced that? Have you ever felt like you were being held back? Or perhaps you have felt like you are too simple and that your life doesn't measure up to the glamorous things other people are doing? Or you assume that because someone else is called to a task that you couldn't possibly be more qualified or more capable.

My tendency is to compare myself to others, and if someone whom I feel is less qualified than I is promoted or given opportunities, I get frustrated with God and demand an answer as to why he didn't choose me. I remember going to a conference one time, and the keynote speaker was a therapist presenting on the topic of depression. As I sat in the audience and listened, I realized my pride was insisting that I could have done a better job, and I should be the one handling such a task.

I have learned that there are many times when God is more interested in shaping my character and teaching me humility than using my skills. However, that goes directly against the world's pressure to stand out and make a name for myself. Our expectations for our lives come from the social norms around us: the messages and examples we receive from the people in our personal lives, what we see on television and in movies, and what we read about in magazines and news articles.[30] We are bombarded with the myth that we must make a name for ourselves, and if we don't, we have failed. There is the additional pressure of feeling the need to be accepted, but again, God's vision for our lives and the world's advertisement of what is best do not always align.

Jesus' announcement that he was the Messiah, as his name suggests, produced a reaction in the people of such anger and hatred that they wanted to kill him. Jesus was not what people wanted or imagined for their savior. Although he was a carpenter, several passages in the Bible metaphorically call him a "cornerstone" (Isaiah 28:16; Psalm 118:22; Matthew 21:42; Ephesians 2:20; and others). Buildings have a cornerstone: a stone that is essential to the foundation, that holds the walls together. Peter used the analogy that the builders rejected Jesus (a stone) and later discovered he was the cornerstone. He was essential to the construction project, and everyone missed it!

The power of rejection on our psychological health is surprisingly strong. Research has shown that social rejection can so affect the brain that it can be the source of physical pain.[31] Even a slight social rejection can trigger hurt, and afterward, the brain works to assess how hurtful and damaging the rejection is. Not surprisingly, it is much more painful to be rejected by someone you love, such as a family member, versus having a stranger or distant acquaintance socially isolate you.[32]

Have you been down that road? For Jesus, the level of rejection was intense. He was rejected by the people in his hometown, the people he had spent years building relationships with. In that culture, family was highly valued, and it would have been socially progressive to leave that part of his life behind.

Jesus warns us, his followers, that we will be rejected by the world (John 15:18–19). As a Christian, it is important that you not equate the world's rejection with your identity. Satan, in his effort to destroy you, will work to have *you* believe society's standards and therefore judge yourself accordingly. Society has all kinds of standards: how much education you have, what you look like, how many friends you have, how much money you make, and how many people follow you on social media. You will not measure up. Thankfully, God does not have the same values. He values people, and his focus is relationship. Jesus did not do life alone. Since he was rejected by his hometown and members of his biological family, he created a new family with the people who committed to following him (Mark 3:31–34). The cost of following Jesus will likely include shifting those whom you are closest to, and that process can be painful and trigger depressive symptoms.

Jesus' life seems to have two very different chapters. We don't know much about what Jesus did for the first thirty years of his life. He must have spent years learning carpentry, working on various building projects, having dinner with his family, and interacting with friends and neighbors. He lived quietly, humbly, and with patience. He left that all behind to begin his public ministry. When Jesus finally reached the pinnacle of his mission, to die for those who rejected him, he carried a wooden cross up to the site of his execution. Upon reaching his destination, he willingly laid himself on the wood and allowed the people he loved to nail him to it. Jesus' final act of love involved wood and nails: the tools of his vocational life.

The stone that was rejected indeed became the cornerstone.

BRING IT TO LIFE

· Have you had personal experience with any of the words
  below? Circle them or write them in your journal.

  Rejected

  Unappreciated

  Worthless

  Overlooked

  Envious

  Insecure

· How does the word(s) you chose directly relate to Jesus'
  life experiences?

· Write out what you believe you need to accomplish to have
  a successful life. Who or what influenced your definition?
  Write what you believe is the definition of the success God
  would have for your life?

· Pay attention to beautiful woodwork around you. Let it
  remind you that Jesus spent the majority of his life in
  the humble business of woodworking. Take the time to
  consider that he knows what it is like to be unseen.

Dear, precious Jesus, thank you for living such a simple life for
years. Jesus, please give me patience for when I feel I am being
forgotten, rejected, or unappreciated. Jesus, remind me of what
goals you have for my life. Remind me that you are not calling me
to a life of glory and honor for myself but to serve others. Show
me how I can serve and promote others. Encourage me to not
find my worth in the things the world glorifies and praises but in
the things you value. Give me patience, confidence, and peace and
show me how I can bring more honor and glory to your name.

Generous Host

PSALM 23; JAMES 1:2–5

Seven years into our marriage, Tim and I reached a pivotal point. We had both made catastrophic choices. Tim joined a business partner who stole the company that Tim had helped build, and the financial losses meant we would lose everything. I had an emotional affair with a man at work and was no longer in love with my husband. We mutually contributed to the destruction of our marriage when just one year earlier our life had seemed beautiful. We had a healthy, happy four-year-old son, Carter. We had bought a comfortable house and remodeled it. We were financially secure and had started the process of adopting a child. How did everything fall apart in one year?

We had to make radical decisions as a result of our financial situation. Tim's brother-in-law generously invited us to stay at a house he inherited; it had been vacant for some time. We would have to move from Minnesota to North Carolina. I did not want to go, but what choice did we have? We sold our newly remodeled eighteen hundred-square-foot home and drove to North

Carolina to move into an eight hundred-square-foot home. Tim assured me the house would be a temporary solution until we could find something more permanent. It was in rough shape, but we could weather it for a year.

The house was originally built in the 1940s, which meant it did not have a foundation. The floors were uneven, and the walls and flooring poorly aligned. The only source of heat was a garage heater in the main room of the home, which served as a living room, dining room, and laundry room. The kitchen was so small that we could not fit a full-size stove into it. Because the house slumped, the stove sat lopsided, and nothing cooked quite right from the uneven distribution of heat. Not to mention the neighborhood had a reputation for being unsafe.

We had to sell a lot of our furniture and household items to make ends meet, so the house was furnished more like a college dorm than a family home. We had one loveseat and a huge bean bag chair. We couldn't afford both a washer and dryer, so we decided to buy a washer and hang our clothes to dry outside.

I could not secure a steady job. I was a substitute teacher at a local Christian preschool and taught horseback riding at a camp one summer. Tim found work at a local factory. It was quite a transition, watching Tim go from owning his own mortgage company to working third shift as a blue-collar worker. We lived on the edge of hunger literally all of the time. Some months we borrowed money from a good friend to buy groceries and then paid him back when Tim's paycheck arrived.

I was deeply angry with God. Where had we gone wrong? We had tithed. We had kept financial promises to him. The Bible said he would bless us. How could anyone call this blessed? God had robbed me of his promises. He moved me away from my beautiful home, my family, my friends, and my life. The words *generous* and *God* did not go together in my mind.

And what about my failing marriage? I was angry with Tim for his poor financial choices, and he was upset with me for my emotional infidelity, but we were forced to be together in that little house every day. It was too small for us to avoid each other. We were too poor to buy things or go places to distract ourselves from each other. And with our finances so tight, we needed each other in order to survive.

Ever so slowly, we inched our way closer to a healthy marriage. Not because of our own spiritual maturity and convictions but because of our sheer need to survive. What started as awkward nights of mostly silence evolved into meaningful conversations and mutual problem-solving for how to get through our tough time. Meanwhile, as our marriage strengthened, the house fell apart. Mice entered the walls through the gaps in the floor. The basement flooded a few times. The pipes would freeze up since there was no heat in most of the house. Tim literally fell through the flooring in the hall one day. It was a constant mess. But gradually, I began to see the redemptive power of that little, broken house.

Because only the living room had heat, the three of us huddled together on the couch on cold nights. Because there was only one living area, we had to agree on the night's entertainment. Because the neighborhood was unsafe, no one went on walks alone. Because the house continually needed repairs, we had to learn to work together to keep it standing. The house was saving our marriage and our family.

What I thought would be a temporary housing arrangement turned into seven years of calling that little house our home. By the time we left, all three of us were truly sad to let it go. Tim and I had fallen back in love inside that little house. Our son, Carter, had fond memories of sleeping in the living room together, playing outdoor games, pinning clothes up to dry outside, and cooking lots of creative dinners.

If God had done what I wanted and defined *generous* in my terminology, Tim and I would possibly be divorced and leading separate lives. God was generous after all. Psalm 23 is an alarming reminder of God's unconventional generosity. David describes the "right path" as being synonymous with the "valley of the shadow of death" (v. 4 NASB). Although he describes the green pastures and the still waters, he also paints a picture of scary twists and turns and acknowledges the fact that we have enemies.

Maybe you are experiencing something similar, and God does not seem generous at all. Maybe he has taken things away from you. Maybe he has deprived you of things you think you need. Maybe the path you are on feels more like a narrow passage through the valley of the shadow of death with enemies waiting for you to trip and fail.

God is generous with his wisdom, love, and intentionality. Sometimes God's most generous acts of love require him to take things from us. Sometimes his most gracious moments are when he leads us into scary places. I will never claim to understand why, but as he says in Isaiah, his ways are "far beyond anything you could imagine" (Isaiah 55:8 NLT).

By allowing us to live in that tiny house for seven years, God radically changed my perspective on my plans, my priorities, and my understanding of the word *need*. Perhaps he is transforming these things for you too.

· Is there something that God has taken away from you that you want back? For whatever you have lost, is God asking you to let him be the One who generously provides for your needs?

· How do you currently define the word *need*, and does it align with what you believe spiritually?

· There are different domains of needs: physical, emotional, mental, and spiritual. In which of those areas do you feel God has not been generous? Seek him on it. Don't be afraid to grieve, to tell him where you feel he has not been generous, and to seek his wisdom, love, and insight. He knows loss is so hard!

Our dear generous God, I pray that you will heal any wounds I might have from not having my dreams, hopes, or wishes granted by you. I pray you will show me specifically how you are working, that you will begin to reveal how your version of being generous is really best for me. I pray that I will find hope in the truth that you give even in the moments when you take away. I don't always understand you. I don't always get why you do what you do. But I beg you to please bring hope and healing. I pray you will grant a picture of your generosity in my life.

The Way

Exodus 14; John 5:24–25; Philippians 1:21–26

I wish I could say that my stay at the psychiatric hospital was the last time I struggled with suicidal thoughts. I wish I could tell you that upon returning home, I started my life over and never struggled again. In a lot of ways, my return home from the hospital was just the beginning of many challenges.

We moved to be closer to my family after my hospitalization, following the recommendation of a therapist who felt that my parents' support would be helpful. We found a church community with which we connected well. I finally found a therapist I felt comfortable with and joined a Bible study and a support group. Gradually, I became more stable and was able to secure a full-time job. We built a townhouse, and I felt like we were starting a new chapter in life.

Still, depression and anxiety pursued me. I would have good days and then spiral into an emotionally, mentally dark place. Tim later told me that he was constantly afraid he might come home and find me dead. I tried to fight off the urges to kill myself, but the thoughts seemed to have a life of their own at times.

I recall one instance vividly. I drove home from work and parked my new truck in our new garage. I closed the garage door. I went inside. The house was quiet, and I was alone. Tim wasn't home yet. It felt like a shadow suddenly crept over me. I felt like the depression would never let me go, and I was tired of living. I started to think of all the ways I had stressed Tim out, how much money my psychiatric care was costing us, how many sacrifices Tim had made to help me survive, and how slow the road to healing had been.

I returned to the garage and climbed into my truck. I sat there holding the key, meditating on how easy it would be. I could just start the truck, leave the garage door closed, and fall asleep. I would be done fighting, and Tim would be free of me. I put the key in the ignition, started the engine, and waited. I thought I would relax and feel at peace now that my life was slowly coming to an end. But then a new voice whispered to me, prompting me to turn the truck off. The problem was that I did not feel at peace living, but I also didn't feel at peace dying. A voice insisted that leaving the world was not the answer. It was a quiet voice but extremely persistent. It kept reminding me of my friend Pat's words: "God will use this." My pain was not meaningless.

Someone suddenly pounded on the garage door. To this day, I have no idea who it was, but the sound yanked me out of my mind, and I realized what I was doing. I pulled the key from the ignition and cried, feeling scared and isolated. I felt crazy, but who could I talk to? Who would understand me? I just wanted a way out. I wanted God to build a bridge that would carry me across the darkness I was in.

The dictionary defines the word *bridge* as "a structure carrying a pathway or roadway over a depression or obstacle." A second meaning is "a time, place, or means of connection or transition."[33] The concept of crossing a bridge implies going over an obstacle, but the word itself can be a verb indicating successfully going from one point to another despite an obstacle. Jesus stated that we cross over from death to life when we believe in him. His death was the bridge that filled the gap that was keeping us from eternity with God. We cross that bridge when we agree to follow him, and we don't accidentally cross back over to being lost when we struggle.

There are times when I have faced harsh situations in my life, and I yearned for God to provide me with a bridge to go over and above it all. What is tiring and frustrating is that God has a pattern of creating a path *through* obstacles and not *over* them. God's version of a bridge, his way and path, tend to not match what seems best to us. In his exodus story, he could have whisked the people up and placed them on the other side of the Red Sea, but he made a way through the water, not over it. God did not leave the people to create their own way; he miraculously provided it. But he had the people take the steps through the passage he created.

The truth is, if you believe in Jesus and you are committed to following him, you have crossed from death to life. When you crossed over, you may have expected to suddenly feel full of daily energy and victory. However, the world, Satan, and our own bodies are so harsh that they can create emotional confusion and make us feel like we are living in spiritual death.

A powerful discovery in my depression journey was the day I realized my suicidal temptations did not mean I was less of a Christian. No, I had already crossed from spiritual death to life! I finally realized God's bridge past the depression was not taking me over it but was a transitional path happening through it. I cling to Paul's words in Philippians: he was looking forward to death. Before understanding this passage, I was afraid to openly share how tired I was of living. Paul chose to stay alive because he knew God's way included Paul living with a purpose. I appreciate Paul's shameless admission that death sounded wonderful. There is no shame in openly sharing that death is the ultimate way that completes our journey.

But you are here now for a purpose. Your life is not an accident; it has meaning. God built the way for your salvation, and you have crossed into that transformation. Now, as you come to the obstacles in your life, the bridges he provides might not look like what you expect. You might find the path through it is long, exhausting, and full of discouragement. Do not let Satan, the world, or your own mind trick you into thinking God has not built a way through it. However, the path might not look like what you expect.

I love that when we talk about going over a bridge, we use the word *cross*. Whatever bridges you are crossing right now, please know that he used a cross so you could safely enter eternal salvation. No one can take that from you!

BRING IT TO LIFE

· Draw a bridge and use the picture to capture the truth that
  you have crossed into eternal salvation and a relationship
  with Jesus and that your new spiritual location is now
  navigating the world with his presence in you.

· What obstacles are you currently facing that you wish he
  would build a bridge over? Reframe it: How does your
  perspective change if he creates a bridge *through* it?

· Notice in the exodus story that God creates the path, and
  the people walk across the riverbeds. There is a team effort
  between God and the people. If you see your challenges
  like the passing through the Red Sea, how can you relate to
  what the Israelites would have seen and felt?

Jesus, our Way through life, I pray to find that you are carving a
path through the pain. Jesus, please provide comfort, strength,
and the supernatural eye to see the purpose in all that is
happening. Jesus, I pray that I will know that you are on my path
with me. You are building a way through my dark moments,
through my dark times, that is much like the passage through the
Red Sea. It is scary, feels unnatural at times, dark, and terrifying,
but Jesus, when you lead the way, give me the courage to follow.

Wind

JOHN 3:1–8

It is interesting to me that a common question in our society is "Where do you see yourself in five years?" I used to have a confident answer, and as the years have passed, with all the twists and turns in my life, I have developed an appreciation for how unpredictable my life has been. As unpredictable as the wind.

To prepare for this devotional, I went and sat at a park close to my home on a windy day and observed the movements around me. It was a bit chaotic. The leaves were blowing in different directions. Some of them landed in the creek rushing by. The trees bent in rhythm and movement to the different gusts that came through. There were moments of calm, and then with a gust, everything around me shifted. And just as Jesus points out, I had no way to predict which direction, when, and how hard the wind would blow. As I sat in it, the picture of my life and experiences were highlighted in my mind. I could relate to the leaves blowing by me.

Wind is essential to the health of our planet. The wind moves things that need to have movement but can't move by themselves. Plants depend on the wind to scatter seeds. In heavy windstorms, dead and dying trees, limbs, and plants are removed to make room for new growth. The wind is essential to climate control. Without gusts of wind, the planet's ecosystems would be like a body of water without a moving current. The world needs wind movement to be healthy.[34] The wind brings new life to things that are dead; it gives movement to things that are dormant.

And so does the Holy Spirit! The Greek word for the Spirit is *pneuma*, which can mean "wind" or "breath."[35] He brings us to life and then often moves us in directions we cannot anticipate. In the New Testament, we read about the Spirit leading Jesus into the desert to have a confrontation with Satan (Matthew 4:1), limiting Paul's ability to share the gospel in Asia (Acts 16:6) and choosing a missionary pair that would later part company due to personal differences (Acts 13:2). The Spirit's decisions do not always follow what appears to be logical. But he is active, involved, and, as we covered earlier, emotionally invested.

I haven't met anyone who doesn't have at least one moment in their life when something happened that pushed them in an unforeseen direction. Can you relate? For me, one of those moments was when I was in college at the University of Minnesota, pursuing a pre-law degree. I had always pictured myself as a lawyer, following in my father's career steps. I took a break from studying one weekend to go to an event hosted by Campus Crusade. It was an opportunity to hear from leaders who were ministering in persecuted churches. As I listened to the testimonies and stories of missionaries and pastors from all over the world, I began processing my plans for my life.

As I left and headed back to my apartment, it felt like the Holy Spirit was climbing into my car with me. I wanted him to leave me alone. I secretly knew my heart's goal was to make money, have a career that would garnish respect, and be successful by the world's standards. I was afraid he might be prodding me in a new direction. My dad invited me to come watch him in court that week. He was trying his case in front of the Minnesota Supreme Court. As I watched my dad and his firm at work, I kept feeling this tug on my heart. It was a nagging feeling that I was not meant to be a lawyer. I continued to resist.

The final push came from my social life. I had recently gone through a hurtful breakup, and my roommate remained friends with my ex-boyfriend. We avoided the topic of him and our old group of friends, with whom I no longer felt I belonged. A few days after the Campus Crusade event, I came home to find my ex-boyfriend and his new girlfriend in my living room with my roommate. It was the final gust of wind I needed. I knew I needed to set a new course for my life.

I shared my thoughts with my parents, who supported my decision to pursue a different career. With only three weeks left in the semester, I began my search for a new university with a reputable, rigorous Bible program. A friend told me about Columbia International University in South Carolina. I went on a campus visit, and at the end of the term, I packed my things and moved south.

I look back now and see a scared girl arriving on campus, where I was struck by the sight of an attentive, kind guy walking a girl. *I want a guy like that*, I thought. Little did I know that one year later, I would be dating Tim Pace, a guy just like the one I had seen on my first day, and I'd later marry him. I also made life-long friends, including a number of professors who changed my life forever.

My feelings of heaviness and depression at that time in my life were serving a purpose, the purpose of convincing me it was time to make a change. I have had other instances in my life when the heaviness of my heart was tied to the lack of movement in my life, and I know the Spirit will likely continue to move me in some way to remove dead growth from my life and plant seeds for new developments.

Sometimes what the Spirit is wanting us to do or what he is making happen defies worldly logic. There are times when his methods seem unkind, unfair, or ridiculous. Like the leaves in the wind, it might seem like chaos. But the Spirit is precise, not chaotic. It seems random to us, but he has a plan! Some people assume the Spirit is in full control and we have no part in life, which can lead to depression and helplessness; others assume all control is in our power and that God is more of a spectator, which can lead to anxiety and feeling overwhelmed. It is important to find the balance, that the Spirit is leading and we are active in following.

Sometimes our depression is part of that equation; it is part of the wind urging us to make changes that we would otherwise avoid. Our depression can also tell us when something is not right. I always assumed my depression was the enemy, but I came to realize that it's a voice telling me that I need to make a major shift in my life. Could your depression be pushing you to change? When you are out for a walk or sitting outside, take note of the wind around you. Let it remind you of the Spirit moving in your life.

BRING IT TO LIFE

- Track the places that the Spirit has taken you. Do you see a pattern or path?

- Draw a sailboat and place yourself on it.

- Imagine the Spirit is the wind, blowing your boat along the course. But he is simultaneously in the boat with you, speaking to you about the direction to adjust the sails. With both roles, he is pushing you in the right direction while also giving you a role in your own story.

- You can move the sails to catch the wind or try to fight it. We all want our boats to have an engine so we could control the direction and speed of our own course, but instead he wants to be the energy moving our life along.

- Is there something you feel the Spirit wants you to do or a change he wants you to make? Sometimes the actions or changes he wants are tough to do. Is something holding you back?

- Has he moved you in directions that were hard to accept?

Lord, help me to follow you even when it's hard to do. Give me insight and wisdom and courage, courage to turn my sails in whatever direction you are calling me to. Lord, I pray for peace and acceptance of whatever painful or surprising twists and turns your direction takes me. May I see what you see. Show me the ways you planted new growth or the decaying parts of me that needed to be removed. Guide me, lead me, and show me how to listen to you.

Artist

PSALM 98:1–8; EPHESIANS 5:19;
REVELATION 5:11–13; EPHESIANS 2:10

Music is complex, mathematical, and very organized. Think about the elements of music: rhythm, pitch, timbre, and volume. Music can also be diverse and surprising. God has created a medium for communication that is much like himself!

The longest book of the Bible is the book of Psalms, which is literally a large collection of hymns. If God asked me what I thought should take up the most pages in his written Word, a songbook would not be my first choice. Yet he saw fit to share his collection of inspired musical creations. The psalms display many elements of theology and bring together a synthesis of the human experience in our lives and our relationship with God.[36]

Research has shown that music directly affects mood. We play fast-paced, lively music at parties and celebrations. We listen to slow, quiet music when trying to sleep. Upbeat music is proven to increase the heart rate and adrenaline levels, whereas music with a slower tempo has the opposite effect. Music has a deep effect on the brain, which is one reason the field of music therapy exists.[37] It also seems to have an impact on the supernatural world. The Bible describes an account of music driving away an evil spirit (1 Samuel 16:14–23). And I love how God's definition of music is not limited to the playing of instruments and singing but also includes the sounds of his creation (see 1 Chronicles 16:33, for example). One of my favorite places to find refreshment is at Bridal Veil Falls in Dupont State Park in North Carolina. The sounds of the rushing water breaking over the rocks soothes my soul. Do you have a place in God's creation that brings comfort? The sounds of waterfalls, the oceans, birds, trees blowing in the wind: it is all music in God's ears!

God loves having his children share in musical experiences together. Paul states in Ephesians 5:19 that we are to sing as a family, sing songs the Spirit has given us. I believe the Spirit is still writing music. The worship songs and hymns people are writing today are still a mark of his creative genius. Music is not limited to our earthly world. The angels sang on the night of Jesus' birth (Luke 2:13–14). The account in Revelation 5:9–11 of humans, thousands of angels and all of creation singing to God is powerful. Picture it: the magnitude and might behind human voices, angels and all creation all singing in unison.

But what does God sing about? You!

In Zephaniah 3:17, the Bible says that God sings over *you*. God has written songs that he sings in rejoicing over the creation of you. Just as parents sing lullabies to their children, so God gets joy from singing to you. I suspect that when you get to heaven, he will play you the songs he wrote just for you, songs that were brought out of his deep love for you. You don't realize how incredibly special you are to the great musician. *You* inspire him.

In the deepest places of my depression, I could never imagine that anything about me was noticeable or enjoyable to God. I was living in the lie that I had to do something impressive to gain his affections and attention. The lie from Satan is that you are not enough, but unlike the world's standards, you are more than enough for God because you were made by him.

God is not just a musician; he creates physical forms of art. In human standards, a great artist is superior in their level of skill, determination, inspiration, and the ability to capture something that is timeless.[38] *You* are the culmination of all those things: you are his greatest achievement.

In art galleries, visitors go to observe the various masterpieces, enjoy their beauty and complexity, and often contemplate what message or emotion each piece evokes. People spend time admiring the talent and skill of a human artist. The art itself does not do anything to get recognition. Each piece has intrinsic value based on the skills of the artist who created it. No one is a more masterful artist than God. God created color, which, like music, has its own structure and design yet flows with diversity and emotion. Blue is known to calm the brain, red brings it to attention, green is soothing, and orange stimulates the appetite. Purple is the hardest for our eyes to see, whereas yellow is the easiest. Even in his design, God gave colors different properties to evoke different emotion.[39]

With his color system in place, God went to work designing and creating wonderful pieces of art. Look at all the varieties in living creatures: mammals, birds, and fish. Think about all the different landscapes, including the various trees, flowers, and edible plants. Look at the sky and marvel at the incredible combinations of colors during both the day and night. Meditate on the different constellations, planets, and the beauty of the sun and the moon. Yet none of it compares to you.

You are a unique piece in God's art gallery. You are a treasured part of his collection, and he delights in being in your presence. He created you with a specific purpose, one which only you can fulfill. God is as personal as he is big. He even knows the number of hairs on your head (Luke 12:7)!

Do not let depression or anxiety misguide you. You are invaluable. Your genetic make-up was one in about seventeen million genetic combinations when you were conceived. God specifically designed you as you are, and he has proclaimed his creation to be good (Genesis 1:31).

How fitting to end this chapter with an excerpt from a song written by David, recorded in the book of Psalms:

> For you created my inmost being;
>   you knit me together in my mother's womb.
> I praise you because I am fearfully and wonderfully made;
>   your works are wonderful,
>   I know that full well.
> My frame was not hidden from you
>   when I was made in the secret place,
>   when I was woven together in the depths of the earth.
>   Your eyes saw my unformed body;
>   all the days ordained for me were written in your book
>   before one of them came to be.
> How precious to me are your thoughts, God!
>   How vast is the sum of them!
>   Were I to count them,
>   they would outnumber the grains of sand—
>   when I awake, I am still with you. (Psalm 139:13–18)

BRING IT TO LIFE

- Take notice of what songs influence you. Do they uplift you or hurt your mood? What song(s) do you most identify with right now? Use music to influence your mood. You can even use different sounds from nature to bring calm and peace.

- Take time to sing worship songs with other believers. Singing in a group promotes good mental health.

- Imagine yourself as a piece of art in God's gallery. Choose a painting or artwork that you feel represents you. What do you notice about the work you chose?

- Read Genesis 1:1–2:1. Spend time observing God's creation. Walk through a garden center and observe the flower varieties, visit an aquarium or zoo and take time to meditate on the skill of our Great Artist, or spend time sitting among his creation and observing all that he has made.

All powerful and masterful Artist, I praise you and thank you for my life. I know that you have created me with precision and care, and you delight in writing songs and singing over me. I pray you will grant me an image of the depth of your affection and love. I pray for a painting, a piece of pottery, a certain item of art that speaks to me and brings to light the idea that I am a priceless work in your art gallery. You love to be in my presence and experience my beauty every day. I pray that awareness will drive away any thoughts or feelings of worthlessness and leave only the joy of knowing you love me. Replace self-doubt with joy!

DAY 16

Fisherman

LUKE 5:1–11; MATTHEW 28:16–20; ACTS 1:8

When my mom contracted Guillain-Barré syndrome, one of the toughest challenges was communication. My mother was unable to speak and could not move any part of her body except to shake her head. The doctors scheduled her for a number of treatments to replace all her plasma. I was helping to care for her in the hospital, waiting for the team of doctors to arrive for her scheduled treatment, when her heart rate suddenly spiked, and her breathing became labored. Her eyes became wild with fear.

I tried to communicate with her and to guess what she might need. "Mom, are you too hot? Too cold?" She shook her head no. "Okay, you seem scared. Would some calming music help?" No. Nothing seemed to calm her. Then the treatment team arrived at the door. When they noticed her rapid heart rate and shallow breathing, they said she needed to calm down before beginning the procedure. I was desperate. "Please, Mom, what is it? What do you need?" She kept thrashing her head back and forth, her eyes pleading with me to figure out what she needed.

I began begging her, "Please, Mom. You must calm down. The doctor is here for your treatment. Please, Mom." Tears threatened to spill from my eyes. The nurse and the doctor also appeared distressed, unsure of how to proceed. Out of ideas, I tried suctioning her mouth, moving her fan, repositioning her legs, but nothing was working. Finally, I fell to my knees at her bedside. "Jesus, please. Please help me. Please comfort my mom. I don't know what she needs, but you do." I continued praying with the nurse and doctor watching.

I felt as if I could physically feel his presence—like he was kneeling on the other side of the bed, holding her other hand, and speaking directly to her. Her heart rate dropped, her body relaxed, and she fell asleep. We all stared at her. The nurse and doctor whispered something, and I began to cry. Wordlessly, as if with new reverence, the team wheeled in the equipment to begin treatment. We had all witnessed what appeared to be a miracle.

Andrew and Peter must have felt a similar kind of desperation. They had been fishing all night but had nothing to show for it. When they met Jesus, he told them to go back out (even though it was the wrong time of day) and drop their nets in the deep side of the lake (even though it was the wrong place to go). Peter told Jesus it did not make sense, but out of respect, he obeyed. What a shock! It worked! I can relate to that moment when you realize all along you were trying on your own, and suddenly, when the Lord guides and directs, things begin happening. Have you had those times in your life? And as Peter and Andrew leave their old life behind to follow Jesus full time, he tells them they "will be catching men" (Luke 5:10 ESV).

Commercial fishing is dangerous. Fishermen die from storms, rogue waves, being crushed or electrocuted by equipment, drowning, and hypothermia. They do strenuous work for long hours in harsh conditions. They obtain their skills on the job, and it is a dangerous job to learn by doing.[40] What a fitting parallel to the life of a Christian.

So often, instead of having the mindset of someone living on a fishing boat, I tend to assume the position of someone on a cruise ship. I look at myself as the consumer of life, and if life doesn't provide for me what seems reasonable and fair, I feel hurt and frustrated. However, the outcome of being on a cruise ship versus being on a fishing boat is also worth noting. Consumers pay to go on a cruise ship, spend time playing and eating, and return home with nothing substantial to show for their efforts. The fishing industry is lucrative with world-wide demand. The work is exhausting, dangerous, and overwhelming, but it is driven by the never-ending need. Do you see the similarities to the Christian life? If you can catch a vision of your part in God's fishing efforts, my hope is that you will develop a new dedication and energy to your daily life.

In the depths of my depression, life didn't seem to have much of a point, but I was looking at life from the wrong angle at that time. I was erroneously approaching my life wanting it to give me something. As I have slowly transitioned my view to what I can put into life, I have found new purpose, meaning, and motivation.

The beauty of Jesus' final command to us before leaving the earth is that he called us to make disciples, which implies making more than just converts. The Bible gives us the short summary of the conversion moments of Peter, Andrew, James, and John, and the rest of the gospel is the long story of the building of their faith. I have met believers who tell me they feel ashamed because they haven't converted anyone to Christianity. But there is so much even beyond a conversion moment. Every person who chooses Jesus will need life-long mentorship. Just as commercial fishermen don't need a formal degree for their position, you don't have to have a theology degree to be an active and important participant in the call of Jesus. The immense job of making disciples involves continual growth for every person, including those who already know him.

And often, I have found that when I am at my wit's end and think I can't go on anymore, the cruelty of my situation magnifies the power of my testimony. The doctors and nurses all witnessed my inability to calm my mom and the impact of one prayer to Jesus. As I sat with my mom for the hour-long treatment after she fell asleep, and born out of the vulnerable moment I had just experienced in the presence of the medical staff, I shared a meaningful conversation with the doctor about my faith. I experienced lot of those vulnerable moments. Because my mom couldn't talk or move, there was no way for her to call the nurse if she needed help. We had believers signing up for shifts to come and care for my mom. All day, Christians were coming and going, filling the hospital with their prayers, baked goods, Scripture readings, and kind words. Doctors, nurses, physical therapists, hospital volunteers, and even the food staff all experienced what sacrificial love looks like.

Shift your viewpoint from seeing yourself on a cruise ship to being a fisherman, someone who is on the high seas with a crew, on a mission to reach people. There are many positions on a commercial fishing vessel: some set the nets and bring the fish in while others keep the ship going by maintaining its equipment; some take care of the crew by feeding and providing medical care, and others coordinate schedules and logs. There is always a captain, who directs the ship and its crew to the best places to find their next catch. And often he takes us places we never thought we would go!

Bring It to Life

- Where do you see yourself, and what role do you think you play in others' lives?

- In what ways can you relate to the life of a commercial fisherman?

- What are your gifts and talents? What do you enjoy doing? Being a part of the mission of saving others can involve any and all talents, from preaching and teaching to having the gift of helping a neighbor rake their yard, writing encouraging notes to someone in distress, or even volunteering to help someone at the hospital. Pray for God to give you the names of people he wants you to reach out to this week.

- We have been called to be God's "witness." Witnesses share what they have seen and experienced. You don't have to be God's lawyer to share what you have seen him do in your life. You don't have to have all the answers to share your story.

Jesus, please help me to trust that you know what you are doing even if I am heading into a huge rogue wave! I pray you will sustain me and help me. Show me all the unique gifts and talents I bring to the team. And give me a vision of where I fit; let me know how needed I am! Jesus, please give me your eyes to see people as you see them. Provide me the strength to keep going as I press on together with those around me.

Lord of the Sabbath

GENESIS 1:28–2:3; EXODUS 16:4–30; MATTHEW 12:1–14

My friends and family know that gifting me money is a bad idea;
I am notorious for spending it on everyday necessities and bills.
For a while, my friends and family encouraged me to use their gift
money to buy something for myself by writing instructions in the
card or expressing their intention to ask me how I had spent the
money. It never worked. I always felt compelled to use it for our
needs. In recent years, my friends and family have changed their
approach and will buy me gift cards to places they know I enjoy
shopping for fun. The challenge to find a way to make me treat
myself has been a long road, but they may have found success!

In a similar way, God created a gift we often use in a way
he did not intend: a day of rest. Back at the creation of the
world, he demonstrated how it works. In his masterful design, he
created our bodies to rest. While some people use this gift as he
intended, others find it difficult to apply in a meaningful way.

I do not like to stop; it feels pointless and irresponsible. At
some point in my marriage, my husband declared that we were

not honoring God since we were not taking a Sabbath day, and therefore, all members of our family were required to take a day off each week. On the surface, I thought that sounded good, and it was theologically sound.

What I didn't anticipate was how hard it would be on my psyche to not work. I felt like an addict coming off drugs. On my first planned Sabbath, I felt like a caged animal. I kept looking at the clock and thinking about all the work that waited for me. I felt like a racehorse, waiting for the gun to go off and the gate to open. I was shocked by my inability to enjoy a day of rest, and as I stepped back and reviewed the experience, I realized I may have stumbled onto a core element of my anxiety. Perhaps it wasn't always the enemy but rather a voice of reason telling me that I was doing too much. Instead of listening, I was reading up on ways to silence it, push through it, and keep going. Why did God design us with such blatant physical limitations?

Science has now proven what God already ordained to be true: Human beings must rest. A reporter with CNN interviewed Dr. Matthew Sleeth, an ER doctor and author of *24/6: A Prescription for a Happier, Healthier Life*, to discuss his findings on how rest impacts overall health. Dr. Sleeth concluded that countries that devalued a stop day have higher rates of depression. Humans are not designed to push through without taking a full day to recharge.[41] The human body will try to compensate for a lack of rest by producing more adrenaline. In addition, we ingest caffeine and stimulants to try to keep up with our own maddening pace. At some point, our minds, emotions, and bodies will buck the system. Dr. Sleeth makes an interesting point that most doctors will ask about diet, stress, and relationships but rarely about work schedules.[42]

God commanded humanity to take one day a week to rest; it is his gift to the world. But in Jesus' day, the religious leaders had taken the Sabbath (which means "cease day") and twisted it into an additional chore, not a respite from daily life. The leaders had weighted it down with rules, twisting it from a day of peace to a day of legalism and judgment.

Jesus is in the business of redemption, not just of people but of all things belonging to him. He rescued the Sabbath and revealed the true nature of it. In his application, Jesus showed that the Sabbath is not static. Just like the money I received for my birthday, whether it is a gift is determined by the receiver. Therefore, if I had gone to the store and bought a six pack of Mountain Dew as a treat for myself, then that would be a gift. But if I was on my way home from work and stopped to get Mountain Dew for my family and decided I might as well use my gift money, then it is no longer a gift. Do you see the difference?

In the Exodus story, all the people had the same job to do each day: gather food for their families. Therefore, the command to stop working and rest was the same for all families. Do you find it insightful (and sad) that some people went out to gather manna to see if God was indeed commanding a day of rest? God is staunch in his defense of his gift; for whatever reason, stopping and resting is an integral part of his design. The decision to stop working is an act of worship. It is a physical way of communicating to God that you trust him to accomplish his plan even if you stop for a day.

In addition to stopping for a day, God instituted sleep— another limitation he has placed upon humans that he, himself, does not need. I have a hard time going to sleep. I stay up late working, pushing up against deadlines. As I crawl into bed, I tend to evaluate my day based on the list of accomplishments I checked off in my head. If I have items yet undone, I may lie awake and strategize how to tackle them the next day. Sleep feels like wasted time. However, like rest, sleep, too, is an act of worship.

To sleep, a person must let their guard down, find an inner place of peace, and agree to let the world keep spinning without cognitively and physically participating in it. It is a physical act that manifests the idea that God is in charge, and we are not.[43] We have to let the world go for at least seven hours a day, or else we experience serious consequences. Studies show that a lack of sleep can lead to emotional disturbances and contributes to depression, risky behaviors, and suicide. A lack of sleep drains the brain's ability to learn, be creative, and solve problems. By allowing our bodies and minds to stop, we experience healing, renewal, and restoration.[44] Without it, our bodies and minds attempt to do the impossible.

Is something keeping you up at night? Go back to the picture of Jesus as your Shepherd. He knows that nighttime is when the flock is most vulnerable. The predators come out, thieves lurk the streets, and darkness makes it hard to see. For that reason, as a good Shepherd, he guides his flock to a safe place, tucks them in, and sits as a watchman throughout the night. He doesn't sleep so that you can.

BRING IT TO LIFE

- What does a Sabbath look like for you? Your work life might not be conducive to stopping, but how can you take time to rest?

- For one week, keep track of your schedule. Review it at the end of the week. Is it possible that your depression and anxiety are speaking to you regarding your hectic pace?

- Below are suggestions from The National Heart, Lung and Blood Institute to aid with sleep:

  > Go to bed and wake up at the same time each day.

  > Have quiet time at least an hour before bed, meaning no TV or computer screen time, no exercise, no large meals.

  > Keep your bedroom quiet, cool, and dark.

  > Avoid nicotine and caffeine. Caffeine can stay in your system for up to eight hours, so avoid ingesting it in the afternoon. [45]

- Pray for those you love who are struggling: imagine wrapping them up like a child and handing them into God's hands while you sleep. Do the same with your life circumstances.

God, thank you for the gift of rest. Help me put my guard down so that I may rest. I pray you will give me a clear picture of you as my Shepherd, leading me to a safe place to sleep. Lord, God, I pray rest will become the gift that unlocks greater health, peace, and knowledge of who you are.

Shield

PSALM 91:4; PSALM 84;
PROVERBS 2:4–8; EPHESIANS 6:16

Anxiety, panic, and disillusionment gain power when the people I love fight with one other. I experienced this when our church went through a season of division. My husband is one of the pastors, and we love our church family. The rift among our friends became a topic of discussion on the internet. It was not that the posts were unjustified, but it was the tragic maligning of our church family that hurt the most. It was seeing strangers engage in my church family's business. It was reading comments and accusations from persons outside the situation that caused more pain and disruption to those church members who otherwise would have continued life without involvement. My head kept reminding me that I was not personally involved in the dispute, but as the momentum gained emotion, my heart felt differently.

I lost sleep, grew agitated, and felt compelled to jump in, demand a cease fire, and save the day. Where was God? I felt like screaming, *Your children are fighting, and you aren't stopping it? Don't you see my church family is tearing apart? Do something!* The anxiety became increasingly unbearable. The rift infiltrated my daily life, affecting my ability to focus on my clients and my kids. The anxiety was gaining on me. It suddenly occurred to me that God is called a shield in so many places in the Bible, yet I felt like I was taking hits over and over with pervasive thoughts and feelings of fear and panic. I took a closer look at the Bible's usage of the metaphor of God as a shield.

In Psalm 91, God's faithfulness is the metaphorical shield. It works like this: If you believe that God is truly good and loves you, then every situation in your life has the potential for good. This powerful picture transforms everything in your life that could be considered negative and reframes it as positive, often in ways you do not know. I do not say this flippantly, nor do I suggest that this practice of reframing is easy. However, it is indescribably liberating when you can redirect your mind to approach your troubles from a positive angle.

In the case of the dispute in our church, I realized God was working in each individual person despite the disagreements. Throughout the wrestling and heartache, I recognized for the first time the depths of my discomfort when it comes to lacking control over the conflicts of others. The moment I set aside my fears and demands for control, I am able to mentally and emotionally slip under the impenetrable shield of God's protection.

Proverbs 2:6–11 gives another perspective on God as a shield: God's words and commands are other ways in which he works to protect us. God does not arbitrarily invent rules for us to follow. Instead, he offers guidance on how we should live. This idea reminds me of the years I cared for horses. My coworkers and I worked hard to establish the pasture as a safe place. We provided plenty of water and hay. We walked around the pasture area, inspecting the ground for anything hiding in the grass that could harm the horses. Our daily care also consisted of socializing the horses and offering exercise to help them stay healthy and develop their potential. Occasionally, a member of the herd would escape, and we'd wrangle the horse back to the safety of the pasture.

In the same way, God sets up fences and perimeters to protect us psychologically and emotionally. He knows the nourishment that our souls need, and his Word keeps us more than adequately fed. God does allow circumstances to stretch us, but they're for our benefit. Staying within the bounds of his guidance and wisdom is a shield from dangers that would otherwise harm us.

In the case of our church conflict, God's words wisely commanded me to remain calm and not respond quickly (James 1:19), to weigh my heart's motives (Proverbs 21:2), and to seek wise counsel (Proverbs 19:20). I am not a wise person. I need God's wisdom to give me insight. I have found that if I follow him, then he will help me make choices that spare me heartache.

Another type of metaphorical reference to a shield is found in Ephesians 6:16. In this instance, our personal faith is our shield among other items that serve as armor against our enemy, Satan. The Greek word for "shield" used in Ephesians is *thureos,* which is a reference to the huge Roman shields that looked more like full-sized doors. These shields were designed to link up with other shields so that soldiers could advance together as a unified group.[46] What hurt most about the disruption within our church was that the links in our shields were being disconnected and tampered with. If you are at odds with a brother or sister in Christ, the pain can cause anxiety because it breaks the lines and detaches your shields.

It is essential that you remember your enemy is Satan. If we stand together, with our shields locked firmly in place and our army united, he cannot break us. If Satan can successfully distract us by having us judge each other rather than holding our shields firmly in place next to each other, then he can break into our ranks and hurt us.

We need a working definition of faith to fully understand what our shield consists of. The author of Hebrews offers one: Faith is "being sure of what we hope for, being convinced of what we do not see" (11:1 NET). Hebrews 11 gives an account of a long list of Biblical characters who maintained faith even though they did not see things come true in this life. It is a summary of instance after instance where, on the surface, it appeared as though God had failed, but in their hearts, each person knew God was keeping his promises despite their life experiences. Satan, your great enemy, will work hard to chip away at your faith in God. Your anxiety might scream that what is happening around you is unfair, which might be true. Nevertheless, do not let your life circumstances dictate your beliefs about God.

It is also essential to establish, promote, and maintain unity among other believers. Strive to hold on to each other and be continually aware of Satan's relentless efforts to divide your faith community. God understands that we must go through this life in community since we are pilgrims in a world that is not our home. In Psalm 84:6, the psalmist describes the pilgrimage through the "Valley of Baka." The English word for *Baka* is "weeping." Essentially, the author writes that as we pilgrim through the valleys of times of weeping, our hearts are strengthened by God, and he provides a life that is not normally found in such a place. [47]

Shield yourself behind the protection of God's faithfulness. Study the Bible and submit to his guidance and wisdom. Don't drop your shield of faith, and keep your arms linked with believers; you need unity to help guard you.

Bring It to Life

· Focus on the character of God and who he is. If you are doubting his goodness, then admit it and seek counsel from others.

· Study the Bible regularly and heed his guidance for your life. Proverbs is a great book for practical advice. Psalm 119 is a great read if you are looking for inspiration on how much God's Word changes lives.

· Stay linked with other believers. This might mean stepping away from disagreements with others who are not essential to our common faith.

Lord God, thank you for shielding me from Satan and his evil schemes. I don't know the struggles I will face in the future, what lies Satan may shoot at me, what challenges I might face, but I pray that I will always trust in your protection. I pray that I will hold fast to my fellow believers and not let go. I pray I will pursue your wisdom because your truths and words shield me from so many troubles that come if I don't follow your guidance. Today, may my mind, emotions, and heart find safety and comfort behind you, my Great Shield.

Brother

JOHN 14:23; GALATIANS 4:3–7;
ROMANS 8:29; JOHN 14:2–3

My aunt is an incredible woman who has been a foster care mom for years. When children stayed with her, she would bring them along to our family reunions and parties. I remember the first time she brought Matthew to a family reunion. He was ten at the time and had recently entered her care full time. I was working in the yard when he sat down to chat with me. As we visited, I had this inexplicable thought: *This child is my son.* I pushed the thought away because Matthew was not available for adoption, and our two previous failed attempts at adoption left me emotionally depleted. I was not about to break my heart a third time.

Every time I saw Matthew over the next few years, I had that same thought: *This is my son.* Matthew's mother eventually lost her parental rights, and he came up for adoption when he was thirteen. However, my aunt explained that only people from his home state were being considered.

We attended a family camping trip, and I watched him play all weekend with the children in our extended family. As we headed home, I told Tim how hard it was not to take Matthew home with us. Tim shook his head and told me we had to stop thinking like that. Neither he nor I could handle another failed adoption attempt. He told me, "Unless someone calls and asks us to adopt him, we have to move on." We agreed we would not discuss it again.

About two months later, I received a call from my aunt, who asked if we were still interested in adopting Matthew. I began to cry and said absolutely. Things had changed, and social services was now ready to consider us. The adoption process involved a lot of paperwork, interviews, and emotional work.

Tim and I took Carter, our only son, out to dinner to tell him the big news. He would be an older brother in a matter of months. As we processed with Carter the implications of our decision, it began to sink in that, of all of us, Carter's life would change most radically. He would now have to share everything he had, including his mom and dad, his grandparents, and his aunts and uncles. Carter's future would forever be altered. Everything Tim and I had to offer would be split in half: our time, love, energy, and inheritance.

Matthew moved in a few months later, and we adjusted to our new life. Carter's daily sacrifices continued. Matthew was not used to being in a family, so we had some difficult conversations, challenging moments, and shifts in the culture of our family. I began to recognize just how much Carter had to sacrifice on behalf of my love for Matthew. If the social worker had told me that the cost of adopting Matthew was to give up Carter, then I would not be able to bear it. I love Matthew and would readily give up everything I have with one exception: Carter.

Jesus is the Father's only son. The Father has a love for his Son that is deeper than any love we can comprehend. Much like an older brother, Jesus chose to accept torture and death to pay for our adoption. It is the greatest love story of all time. I made a mistake in thinking that Jesus' sacrifice ended there, but in a way, his death was only the beginning of his payment for us. Jesus now shares with all of us not only his Father but also all of the benefits of being in a relationship with God. We are difficult children. We are rebellious, defiant, and selfish. Jesus is incredibly patient with us!

After the state of Iowa agreed to let us adopt Matthew, we had a lot of preparations to make before his arrival. We had to get Matthew's room ready. Carter graciously helped us put together Matthew's new bedroom furniture and decorate. Carter and his friends went through their clothes and donated anything they thought Matthew would like. In the same way, Jesus has been preparing our heavenly home for us. In John 14:2, Jesus says that the Father has a house for all of us, and we have a place set aside that belongs to us. What an incredible picture!

We sent Matthew a survey before he moved in to learn about his favorite things. When he returned the list, we bought decorations and colors that matched his favorite sports teams and hobbies. We excitedly put it all together and waited (impatiently) for the day when he would open the door and take in the visual representation of our love for him. And so it is with your heavenly big brother, Jesus! He is preparing a place for you!

I once had a dream in which I experienced some of Jesus' preparations. In my dream, I died from a car accident. I left my body and approached heaven. Jesus stood there waiting for me, dressed in glowing gold and white robes, and his eyes were flames. He jumped up and down in excitement, exclaiming how much he had been looking forward to my arrival. Then he brought me to a place he had specially prepared for me. My favorite dog and my favorite animals were there, and it was beautifully designed to resemble my favorite places on earth. What took me by surprise was Jesus' excitement. But now that I have experienced adopting Matthew and the impatience of waiting for him, I understand only a fraction of how Jesus must feel waiting for us.

Someday I will be home, but right now my mission is to bring as many people with me before I go. Satan may try to use your depression to rob you of your zeal for life. He might try to get you to focus on death and leaving the world early, to chase after the place Jesus has prepared for you. Instead of listening to that string of lies, I encourage you to follow the example of your big brother, Jesus. Just as he unselfishly lived and died to rescue you, follow in his footsteps and pursue others to bring them into our spiritual family. Adopting Matthew has been a dream come true that also required sacrifices. You bring the Father so much joy when you invite people who are already in his heart to join our spiritual family. You are needed!

I continue to notice how Carter is a daily picture of Jesus in our home. This summer, we traveled to North Carolina, where we had lived for many years and where Carter had grown up. During our trip, we hiked to High Falls located in Dupont State Park, which we had visited many times years before. As we approached the waterfall, Carter and I walked the familiar path, but Matthew was hesitant and unsure. He had never seen a waterfall. As I watched the boys, I saw Matthew stop and Carter turn around to talk to him. Then I saw Carter take off his shoes, step on the rocks, and lead Matthew by the hand. With each step, Carter went first, then turned around, grabbed Matthew's wrists firmly, and helped him take another step. Eventually they reached the falls and stood at the base in awe.

Jesus has walked the path of our lives and knows each and every step. When we approach a path we have not yet trekked, Jesus graciously takes off his sandals, steps into the cold water, and firmly holds on to us. Step by step.

Bring It Home

- Read Luke 15:11–31, the familiar story of the Prodigal Son. Even though we tend to focus on the lost son and the father, the elder brother also plays a central role. In biblical times, it was appropriate for an older brother to rescue a younger one on behalf of the father. What stands out to you in this story?

- Imagine if Jesus were inserted into the story. How would it read differently?

- Listen to "Love Song" by Third Day. How does this song conceptualize today's concept?

To my loving elder brother, thank you for rescuing me. Thank you for giving up so much to save me and bring me into your family. Guard me from Satan, who will want to tempt me to depart this world early. Instead, give me the eyes to see those in need of rescue and the zeal you have in seeking and saving the lost.

DAY 20

I Am

EXODUS 3:1–15; 6:1–9; REVELATION 1:8, 4:8

My dad has colon cancer, and preliminary tests indicate it is quite extensive. Cancer diagnoses often lead to periods of waiting: days, weeks, months, and years. During a long week of waiting, I found myself on the internet, googling terms like "survival rates of colon cancer" and "treatments for colon cancer." I read through medical websites and familiarized myself with the variety of treatments.

Suddenly, I stopped, took a psychological step back, and asked myself what I was doing. I was attempting to take matters into my own hands. I was not going to wait for the doctor to break down the severity of the cancer and explain treatment plans. All of the internet searches in the world could not give me the answers I truly wanted, so why was I wasting so much time doing it? What comfort was it providing me? I was desperately searching for any grain of information that would calm my anxiety. I wanted to feel a sense of control. I wanted the medical data I had read to convince me that everything would be fine.

The problem with that approach is that, because of my anxiety, I tend to disregard whether the likelihood for danger is imminent or slight. My anxiety screams negative outcomes at me even when the odds favor good news. My anxiety tells me it is critical to prepare for the worst, lest I be caught off guard. But our mind, body, and emotions are not designed to live in a constant state of worry. Fear itself isn't bad for our system; in fact, it is designed to help us survive. In a moment of fear, the blood flow increases to our core muscles, giving us more strength. Hormones and neurotransmitters send a surge of adrenaline and messages to the entire body to make it more alert. Digestion slows down as well as our focus on memory, language, and logic. This intense drive is only helpful in dangerous situations where this kind of energy is essential for survival. Experiencing this level of fear over a prolonged period begins to wear on the body, mind, and emotions. [48]

I have lived my life preparing for the worst possible outcomes. Sometimes life has felt like a line of elevators, all of which can carry me to different floors of trials and pain. Although the doors shut for some people, all my elevator doors are slightly cracked open, leaving me to believe that one will suddenly open, and I will be forced inside at any given time. The problem with that mindset is that it is exhausting. It's mental training for things that never come to fruition. Is it even possible to truly prepare for your worst nightmare? I used to have a sign in my office that read, "To those who look behind your shower curtain for a murderer: If you do find one, what's your plan?"

Most people attempt to comfort me by trying to convince me that the likelihood of danger is slight, but this approach is ineffective because however unlikely the worst might be, my brain knows that it is still possible. So while others pass through their mental halls of elevators, representing all manner of possibilities, their doors remain closed until something actually happens. Mine are always cracked open, leaving just enough room for me to imagine. The truth is that the preliminary images of my dad's colon do not look good. The doctors are moving quickly, but we have no definite answers and no way to prepare for whatever lies ahead.

Moses and the Israelites must have felt the same uncertainty. The exodus story is an incredible account of God's mighty power, freeing an entire nation from bondage and slavery. As God presents himself to Moses and when Moses' courage begins to falter, God uses the name "I AM" to represent his unlimited power and might.

This name choice intrigues me. If God were to ask me to do something terrifying, then I imagine he'd assure me with a name that conveyed aggression, power, or might, but he chose "I AM." The name parallels "the One who needs no introduction." The One who has so much history of greatness and majesty that he needs no explanation. To prove it, God listed the ancestors of the Jews, who each had their own profoundly miraculous encounter with the great I AM. He was reminding Moses and the people of his proven track record.

After Moses began his conversations with Pharaoh (all of which did not go well), the Jewish people refused to be comforted. The book of Exodus records their response as one of people who would not listen "because of their discouragement and harsh labor" (6:9 NIV). I imagine they had overwhelming feelings of despair, that there was no way out. God's name "I AM" is built on the truth that he is the God who brought about incredible works of the past, who controls the present, and who has already mapped out the future.

God knew the Israelites had to plant their emotional stakes into the strength of his name because matters would only intensify. The Bible records the growing battle between the I AM and the gods of the Egyptians. Drawn out over months, the battle involved dreadful plagues that became increasingly extreme. The end times will resemble the ferocious battle between the I AM and the forces of evil in Exodus. When the world comes to an end, the I AM has recorded in Revelation that the constant comfort of his people will be the knowledge that God will always be—at all times and in all spaces. Once we physically live with him, we no longer experience physical, mental, or emotional pain (Revelation 21:3–7).

To apply it to my modern-day struggle, I find comfort in the knowledge that even if the elevators of my worst nightmares slide open and I am forced into frightful scenarios, then the great I AM will be inside the elevator, waiting for me. As I stumble in, terrified, he is already there to catch me, steady me on my feet, and remind me to hold on to him when the elevator inevitably drops. Beyond his track record in the Bible, the I AM has built a track record in my personal life. I have seen him do incredible things, especially during the moments when I was too discouraged to secure my faith in him. Notice that in Exodus, God was still determined to free his people, even if they would not listen and believe in him.

As I pray about my dad's battle with cancer, my prayers are focused on the minds, emotions, and spirits of my family and me. If and when we find ourselves in a medical crisis, I pray that all of us quickly and firmly cling to Jesus, feel him steady us, and hear him say, "I AM...who is, who was, and who is to come" (Revelation 1:8 TPT).

Bring It to Life

· Think about God in your past, present, and future. Write out the ways in which God has been in your past and how he is showing up right now. Meditate on how you can trust that he is in your future.

· The next time you find yourself standing before a hall of elevators, let them remind you of the metaphor of all the possibilities of life and that God is already in the elevator in you find yourself.

· I am. The beauty of this name is that it provides the unique perspective that God is whatever your soul needs. When you write the words "I am," you can attach whatever words you need to describe him. For example:

  ➤ "I am your protector."

  ➤ "I am your provider."

  ➤ "I am your comforter."

· Write your own "I am" statement about God that applies to your circumstances.

The great I am, I pray that I will live in the freedom of knowing that nothing takes you by surprise and that you are ready and willing to comfort and encourage me in my time of need. I pray you will work in my heart to bring healing and restoration and peace, a peace that can't be taken from me. I pray for the future, and I pray I will hold tight to your steady hand.

DAY 21

Warrior

PSALM 18:1–36; LUKE 12:4–5;
EPHESIANS 6:10–18

The Marine Corps has what is called the "warrior's ethos."
It reflects their mindset about war, and it dictates how they
train their troops. One training motto is that it is "better to
sweat during times of peace than to bleed during times of war."
Although a large percentage of Marines are not actively deployed,
the philosophy taught during boot camp is that as long as the
enemy is alive and active, every solider is on duty, even if not
actively engaged on the front lines.

Underlying each of these aforementioned beliefs is the concept of unity. The Marines specifically teach that each individual
is part of a larger picture. They are trained to sacrificially give in
order to preserve the success of the mission. And a clear understanding of the enemy is essential.[49]

If you are a follower of Jesus, then you are literally at war.
Your great enemy, Satan, hopes that you will not be mindful
of the war you are in. Satan is crafty and knows the Bible well,

probably better than we do. But unlike us, he does not have the Spirit to to lead him. The comfort we have is that our God is a mighty warrior who is terrifying when angry or provoked. The description of his aggression and zeal in Psalm 18 is a poignant picture of a God who is fearless and defensive of his children. Unfortunately, we often misunderstand the war we are in, and we get depressed or anxious when it seems like God is not defending us or keeping us safe like we think he should.

I have had times in my life when I was truly wronged. I have yet to meet someone who has not been the victim of a wrongdoing that affected them physically, emotionally, mentally, or spiritually. The question then arises: Where is God? I have had many clients ask, "God could have stopped it, so why didn't he?" This is a valid question that I, or anyone else, cannot answer flippantly. I suspect it is a question all Christians will face at some point in their lives. For me, the key to unlocking the answer to that mystery goes back to identifying who my enemy is and who my enemy is not.

Jesus states in Luke 12:4–5 that we do not need to fear people. People cannot injure us in eternity. However, the one who is to be feared is our enemy, Satan. He is the one who can cause eternal terror. Satan is the one who is on a warpath to keep people from God. He is the one who can use circumstances, people, and the world around us to wreak havoc on our spiritual health.

I have seen guilty and evil people thrive. But I am not at war with other people. I am a soldier fighting a very real, physically unseen enemy, who is extremely dangerous and hopes that I will focus on other humans instead of him.

Depression and anxiety thrive under the false assumption that your enemies are other people because there is a sense of despair when the wicked flourish and the innocent suffer. Pursuing justice on this earth is extremely important, and we should advocate for those in need. However, it's also important that we remain aware that justice in this life is not guaranteed.

My most difficult battle in this arena involved a group of boys who sexually assaulted me on the playground during recess when I was in first grade. I remember telling my teacher, who took me into the hallway and instructed me to never tell anyone. I can still feel my back against the wall and see her kneeling in front of me, explaining that it was inappropriate for me to tell anyone because she would handle it. I pushed it out of my young mind, a common survival method for a young child who has suffered trauma.

But in my teen years the memories came flooding back to me. I quickly realized that her decision to keep me silent was driven by a personal motive; if I spoke up, then she would have to account for her failure to keep me safe. Anger and hurt raged inside of me, but I had nowhere to put it. For years I wished I could track down each one of those boys and pursue some sort of justice. But I had no way of locating them or my first-grade teacher. I fantasized about what it would be like to show up at her door and publicly shame her. Under the weight of my anger and grief, my depression grew.

Once I was able to walk through the truth that this memory does not control me and cannot steal my faith, my life changed. I may not be able to explain why this awful experience happened to me, but I live in the freedom of knowing that God is not blind. He sees everything that happens, and my heart and mind are kept safe in his strength.

Since the war in this life is against Satan, I am keenly aware that the battles I face are happening in my mind and heart, and I see the evil he promotes all over the world. He loves all kinds of crime, deceit, lies, and violations against the innocent. But what he delights in even more is defaming God and driving people away from a loving relationship with their Creator.

Jesus is recorded as getting angry and verbally attacking the religious leaders of his day because they kept the innocent from God (Matthew 23). He relentlessly confronted anyone who defamed God's name by misrepresenting him. The Bible records Jesus physically driving out people who were cheating those who sought to make sacrifices to God (John 2:12–22). His passion for all to have access to eternal life cannot be understated.

God hates when people are wronged. He hates all forms of evil. And even though we might not see justice served within our human life, it doesn't mean that God doesn't have plans for how to make it right in our next life. You aren't guaranteed victory when fighting other people in this life, but you are guaranteed victory over Satan. It is not easy, and the war often gets harder as you grow older.

Members of the military are expected to continually learn new skills, advance their ranks, and maintain their physique. The life of a soldier means a life of continual growth with no point of arrival. The growth is hard work and requires discipline, training, and humility.[50] In the same way, you need to always be in training, maintaining your spiritual health, and preparing every day for Satan's attacks. Even when life is peaceful, we need to be ready to use the tools God describes in Ephesians 6:10–18.

We are called to fight for justice and be advocates for change in our world (Micah 6:8). We are called to stand up for the vulnerable, care for the needy, and push for positive, healthy change. At the same time, we must live with an understanding that our emotional and mental health cannot be determined by the justice (or lack thereof) in this world.

If a lack of justice is a core piece of your depression or anxiety, try to rest in the knowledge that God is not blind and does not ignore wrongdoing. Focus on your true enemy: Satan. Humans can harm our bodies and attack our minds, but they cannot destroy our souls.

Bring It to Life

- Look up Ephesians 6:10–18 and list in your journal the armor of God.

- Picture each of these elements. Which one(s) do you feel the weakest in right now? What do you feel you need to do to strengthen your armor?

- Think for a moment about a person whom you currently consider an enemy. How is Satan using that enemy in your life?

Our Mighty Warrior, thank you for giving me the Bible, which is my defense against my terrible enemy, Satan. I pray you will show me the ways Satan is trying to attack me today and open my eyes to the ways he is craftily trying to infiltrate God's ranks. Instead of fear, give me boldness, wisdom, discernment, and guidance. Encourage me when I see evil thrive in the world around me and keep my heart from despair. Rescue me from Satan's evil schemes and protect me.

Bread and Living Water

JOHN 6:35, 53–58; DEUTERONOMY 8:1–5;
MATTHEW 6:9–13; JOHN 7:37–39

I know a boy who, at the age of nine, was determined to find God. While growing up, his mom struggled with addiction, and he and his brother were moved around continually, sometimes living with his grandma or in a treatment center with his mom. He told me how he remembers the day when he was called out of class at school and found a social worker waiting to talk to him. The social worker explained that he was being moved to foster care. They proceeded to take him home to pack up his belongings and dropped him off at his new temporary home, where he lived for three years.

As he continued attending school, he met a classmate named Luke. Luke was kind and invited him to church. He had never been to church, and on his first visit, he immediately felt drawn to the teaching, worship, and community. As time went on, his mom became worse, not better. As his family deteriorated, his internal drive to know God grew. Luke stopped going to church for a period, but that did not stop the boy. He attended regularly, getting rides from people from the church or his foster mom.

His biological mom eventually permanently lost custody, and he described how the new, uncharted territory of adoption lay ahead of him. He was thirteen at that point and aware that most adoptive families are uninterested in pursuing an older child as opposed to a baby or a toddler. He went to church more to find confidence and strength in God as he waited to find out what his future might hold.

This precious boy, Matthew, is now my adopted son. Matthew's spiritual hunger continues to drive him to know more about Jesus. One night at a youth event, the speaker asked each attendee to talk about the moment they realized their need for God. It was an honor to hear Matthew tell his story and how, as a child, he had built a special bond with Jesus.

Our spiritual beings are aligned with our physical bodies. We cannot survive without food and water. Therefore, Jesus harnesses the physical body's needs and describes himself as bread and the Spirit as water. The physical body not only needs food but also continual nourishment. It is important to have an eating routine instead of waiting to eat until your body is starving with hunger. If your body is telling you it's hungry, then you need to feed it. The more you ignore the cues and signals of your body, the less in tune you will be with it.

It is also essential to pay attention to what you are putting into your body. Eating junk food makes you feel nourished for a short period of time, but it doesn't last and only gives the illusion of nourishment. Your body is meant to eat slowly and enjoy food. Even taking in the aroma of food is good for the body and promotes health.[51]

Jesus' discussion of the needs of the physical body provides a powerful parallel we can follow: if you are hurting, depressed, and anxious, then it is likely your spirit sending the message that you are spiritually malnourished and that you need him.

When I am most weak and vulnerable, I sometimes erroneously seek nourishment from distractions like TV or the internet. Those practices are not necessarily sinful, but they are not a spiritual substitute. Those sources cannot give me the spiritual vitamins and minerals needed to sustain me. I struggle with making time to be with Jesus. My life gets so jam-packed with work, relationships, and obligations that I allow interruptions to take up my time for the Bible. When I'm invited to Bible studies or focused time with other believers, I admit that a movie sometimes sounds a lot more appealing.

Still, I recognize that as life becomes more stressful and hard times more frequent, my need for spiritual nourishment often doubles or triples. I get stretched to my limit, much like athletes or soldiers whose bodies require a lot of protein and calories to meet their physical demands. As you already know, you are a soldier at war. You need a lot of spiritual nourishment. Psychological strain is our spiritual hunger cue.

In the Old Testament, the Israelites wandered in the desert. To feed them, God literally rained down food for them, which they went out and gathered each day. As the book of Deuteronomy explains, God knew this daily dependence on him was a way to grow their spiritual depth. He provided the nourishment, and they went out to receive it. In the same way, God provides spiritual nourishment, and it is our responsibility to gather it, just like the Israelites gathered their food each day. Jesus said to ask God for "daily bread" when teaching his apostles how to pray. Although I am sure he was referring to the physical body, I also believe he intended us to seek daily nourishment for the spiritual body.

Just like we need nourishment, we also need water. The Spirit is called "living water" that springs up within us (John 4:13). We need daily hydration. As we take in the Bible, the Spirit shows us new things. He is living with us, a person who is daily coaching us with the nourishment we are taking in.

There are times when we can't feed ourselves and need help from other believers. In the darkest parts of my depression, I could not think clearly. I felt like I was in a mental fog. During that time, Pat, my mentor, would come and tell me Bible stories and explain the applications. She turned the pages of her Bible to different promises and explain what they meant. She helped me understand that just because I was struggling to take in God's nourishment, it didn't mean I was too sinful to hear God's voice. I just needed help. But I didn't know what to pray. Pat prayed over me and with me. She articulated the needs of my weak heart. It was the physical equivalent of someone shifting the rocks to a dammed-up creek. The internal water flow was still there; I still had the Spirit in me. But my mind had blocked access, and Pat was pushing aside the barriers to make way for my parched soul to drink in the life the Spirit gives. There is no shame in needing help.

For my beautiful son, Matthew, now that he is safely living in our home, I pray that he will still seek out the nourishment of Jesus and drink in the wisdom of the Spirit. I hope that neither he nor I will need psychological pain to remind us of our spiritual needs. That is my prayer for you too.

Bring It to Life

· Take a minute to examine your spiritual eating habits. When comparing them with the parallel of physical eating habits, is there something that stands out to you that you need to change? If so, what? Do you need others to help you right now?

· When you eat physical meals, take time to mentally note if you have had enough spiritual food for the day.

· The bread of the Bible comes in different flavors: hymns, stories, parables, letters, prophesies, and teaching, just to name a few. What would resonate with you most right now? Think about ways you can catch spiritual "snacks," like Christian music, daily devotionals, and text threads with other believers. Get creative!

· Create a spiritual meal plan that includes both individual time in the Word and time with other believers.

Jesus, as I am on this journey of life and need so much nourishment to sustain me, show me how to fight for time with you. Show me new ways to get my daily spiritual needs and not to allow anything to stand in the way of it. Do not let Satan shame me out of spending time with you, but may I have a desire that comes from enjoying you. And when I need others to help me, give me people who will bring me spiritual meals and help me get the nourishment I need.

DAY 23

Potter

ISAIAH 29:16; JEREMIAH 18:1–6;
ROMANS 8:20–21; 2 CORINTHIANS 4:7–11

People often quote the Scriptural metaphor of God as a potter (Isaiah 64:8), so I looked forward to exploring more on this name of God. What I did not anticipate was the depth and implications of this metaphor that God has chosen for himself. I researched the ins and outs of a potter and quickly became overwhelmed. Pottery is complicated; it is the perfect blend of science and art. One expert described it as requiring "physical skills, scientific knowledge and creative thought."[52]

As I struggled to understand the process of pottery, I discovered the vast and seemingly endless number of details and variances from which a potter must choose in order to craft each work of art by hand. The decision about what to create is only the beginning. Who knew there were so many different types of clay, with different amounts of elements within each one? It turns out that clay differs based on where it is extracted from the earth. Components like silica and quartz directly affect the degree of heat that the potter needs when firing as well as the speed of cooling the product.[53]

I attempted to understand the chemicals involved, but frankly, it was too complicated for me to comprehend. And that was just learning the basics of the various types of clay. Never mind trying to grasp the different types of glazes, textures, and kilns.[54] I became lost in charts and graphs on heating levels, interacting with the colors, patterns, and textures. The potter infuses culture, purpose, and meaning into the details he or she chooses to use.

In Jeremiah 18:1–6, we read an account in which God sent Jeremiah to a potter's house to watch the artisan in the process of making a pot. God wanted the prophet to watch the process unfold as God explained its application: humans are not god; only God is.

Successful potters set out to personally design and create a product that is both beautiful and practical.[55] What a perfect description of our God! The clay, our human bodies, are akin to the pottery, born out of his meticulous planning, both in science and art form. It is no secret that our bodies are complicated but not identical to one another. Even in an instance where twins share identical DNA, research shows that it does not mean they share the same personality or interests. Each human (each piece of art) is both a biological marvel as well as a unique artistic design.

Unfortunately, our society largely defines what is beautiful and what is not. Sadly, media images are doctored to produce visual representations of human beauty that are physically impossible.[56] Under pressure to match perfection, people make huge sacrifices in their quest for what they cannot obtain, giving time, money, and the cost of their own health to strive for beauty. Research has shown that this drive toward perfectionism is directly linked to depression.[57]

But beyond beauty, we also face the reality that sometimes people are born with biological flaws. Beautiful souls are born into bodies that are not functional, have deficits, or provide challenges that are difficult to accept or overcome. Even if we aren't born with biological challenges, our bodies wear out over time. Much like the ancient pottery seen in museums, it is clear that daily use and the passing of years break down our physical containers, eventually releasing our souls back to God.

God does not make mistakes, and the body he designed for you was carefully put together with extreme attention to detail. However, that is not meant to imply that it is easy to accept the bodies we are given. Depression can feast on the disconnection between the mind and body with the mind continually shaming the body, thus leaving emotions tormented with discontent and sadness. Regardless of the source of disappointment and pain, it is important to understand that even our broken bodies are part of God's design.

The flaws of our bodies can enhance our spirit, which is the piece of us that is eternal. The more our temporary body fails us, the more we yearn to go on to the next life. And, as we know, the aging process will unravel the physical body.

The word *homesickness* was first used in the 1700s and was created to refer to the physical distress a person feels over being separated from home or anticipating a separation.[58] The aging process prepares us for our next adventure, making us spiritually homesick. It reminds us that this is a temporary stop to our permanent resting place. Your beautiful spirit, which God made to mirror his own, was poured into your temporary and carefully crafted work of art. The goal is not for the exterior to be the idol of perfection or for it to last forever but for it to carry you through this temporary, short life. In comparison to eternity, the body you are in is merely a pit stop.

God celebrates you, his hand-made piece of art. Satan, on the other hand, hates God and delights in destroying anything God celebrates. Satan revels in our discontentment, but even in our discontentment, we can find hope. I will admit that I myself have had many conversations with God about my frustration not over my own body but over the health of my husband's body. My husband has a rare brain condition that has required multiple brain surgeries and will require more surgeries in the future. He continually encounters new handicaps and suffers from severe migraines as well as trouble with his memory. Because of his physical limitations, Tim must depend on God to do his job as a pastor at our church and to get through his daily life.

However, so much beauty can be found in recognizing how God overcomes those handicaps and uses Tim despite his health challenges. I hear him preach and witness firsthand how powerfully God uses his message. I sit in awe of the work of the Spirit, and I realize that because of Tim's condition, I know with certainty that God wrote the message and delivered it through Tim. It's the image of a cracked pot that somehow holds water perfectly; there is no doubt that something supernatural is taking place.

Another important application is to not compare yourself to other artwork. I have clients who tell me they feel weak because they know other people who are going through similar circumstances, and those people seem so much stronger. The truth is that those other people might indeed be stronger. Each of us has different weaknesses and different strengths that make us unique.

In a beautiful twist of genius, God not only specifically takes time to design our bodies, but he also writes a specific story surrounding our physical experience. Imagine a potter sitting at his wheel, carefully forming his creation, already knowing exactly how it will be used and what this piece of art will endure.

God has seen it all! Someday, when we arrive in heaven, we will understand the role our bodies have played in our experiences on earth as well as the nature of the twists and turns we experienced. Until then, meditate on the idea that the great and masterful Potter, who is both scientist and artist, has carefully designed you and your life.

BRING IT TO LIFE

- Read Psalm 139. This psalm brilliantly blends the concepts that our bodies and our life stories are in the Potter's hands. Reflect on what stands out to you the most.

- Visit an art gallery or shop and observe the distinct varieties of pottery. If possible, watch a potter at work. It is amazing! Meditate on the focus and dedication the potter must have in creating his or her masterpiece.

- How do you view your physical body? What challenges do you face in accepting it?

Our great Potter, I pray I will see my body and the twists and turns in my life as you see them, you who not only creates individually designed pieces of art but who also sees all the ways your art is used. Guard my heart and mind from Satan, who longs to have me feel discontent and frustration. Give me eyes to see myself as you see me.

The Word and the Light

JOHN 1:1–14; GENESIS 1:1–3; PSALM 119:105–107

John opens his Gospel by explaining that Jesus was the *Logos* (which means "thoughts expressed verbally and in writing") of God, which existed from the beginning. The word *beginning* here actually refers to timelessness. It is a word that is equivalent to the idea that Jesus was the physical manifestation of the eternal thoughts of God, which have always existed. The *logos* was not only expressed through Jesus but is also present in the written words of the Bible, which record God's first spoken words: "Let there be light" (Genesis 1:3 NIV). Although his words were literal and brought forth physical light, I believe his words had a secondary meaning. I believe this was also the beginning of God revealing himself, as if to say, "I will now be known!"

In numerous places as you read the Bible, the Word and the light go hand in hand. In John 8:12, Jesus declared, "I am the light of the world. Whoever follows me will never walk in darkness, but will have the light of life" (NIV). The following of Jesus involves interaction with the Word: the voice of God *is* the light.

Light is an effective physical phenomenon that exhibits important dimensions of God. Darkness cannot overcome light. Light can be seen from far away and gets brighter and more brilliant the darker the surroundings. Light brings illumination. It provides clarity. When my husband travels without me and I am alone in my house overnight, I leave the lights on. I feel safer being able to see everything around me. If I keep the lights on, then it is less likely that something or someone will sneak up on me and catch me unaware.

Our souls are much the same. God's words are the light, and Jesus shone the brilliance of God and all his thoughts. He was transparent in his anger, fear, joy, grief, and love. He was merciful, full of compassion, and innocent. He was kind, humble, and incredibly brave. Each day that he walked the earth, everyone interacting with him experienced the fullness of God. But in addition to Jesus being the human manifestation of God, the Spirit authored the Bible, which chronicles the thoughts and the full essence of who God is. The Word is the lamp that guides us through this unsafe world (Psalm 119).

Jesus calls us to step into his light, into the authentic and transparent existence of vulnerability, which does not come naturally. He asks us to take in his teaching and draw near to him, and in turn, to allow him to illuminate what is within us. The hardest part of this process sometimes involves allowing others to see the secret things we keep locked away.

Secrets hold a dark power that prevents us from experiencing all that God is. Living with secrets can harm us both psychologically and physically. Living a lie is emotionally expensive; it can lead to anxiety, stress, and depression. Working to conceal something can also cause higher blood sugar levels, stomach issues, and higher heart rates.[59] We are not meant to live in the darkness of secrets. But people who live with secrets are often afraid to set aside whatever façade they have built for fear of rejection and judgment. Sometimes their secret holds power because its revelation would lead to difficult situations, conversations, or consequences.[60]

If you are experiencing depression and anxiety because a hidden piece of you holds you captive, then God wants you to step into the light, to bring your darkness before him and even before select others. He is the *Logos,* which is "truth," and he has promised that if you hold to his teachings, you will be set free (John 8:32). *Free.*

Transparency can be harmful if we do not experience it in the manner that God has designed. As he is with all of God's beautiful gifts, Satan does not want you to be vulnerable. If Satan can trap you into a secret that you carry in shame, he can isolate you more easily. Depression and anxiety thrive in the darkness of lies, much like mold that grows in damp, dark places. The Light of the World, shining through the Word of God, longs to shine into those secret places and bring warmth and healing.

The first step to overcoming secrets and lies is to be honest with God. In the moments of my life when I lived a lie, I hid from God, much like Adam and Eve after their original sin (Genesis 3:8). But he already knows your heart and mind. He is aware of all you have done. He wants you to *choose* to step into the light. Talk to him; use verbal words or journal writing or even drawings. Express your experiences to the God who loves you.

The second step is to share your burden with another person, even if it is just one. Satan can use others to bring shame and guilt when we long to find and share our lives with someone. Since it is both healthy and important to share your life with others, you will want to have at least one person with whom you can safely share your secrets.

How do you determine who is safe and who is unsafe? Unsafe people come in different forms. Some unsafe people avoid vulnerability and close relationships because they themselves are living a lie. Others are unsafe because they are judgmental in nature, much like the Pharisees of the Bible. Although they may appear to have their act together, their hearts do not shine with the power of God's grace and truth. The third category of unsafe people are those who are too irresponsible to be trusted. These people are takers who demand your care but are unable or unwilling to return the care.[61]

Safe people shine the light of Jesus. They carry the beautiful combination of grace and truth, and both elements must be present in order to be true light. Safe people congregate in common places. Churches that are full of grace and truth have pastors and leaders who are vulnerable with their congregations about their failings and their need for Jesus. Churches that understand Jesus will have some sort of community that encourages relational connections.

Another place to find safe people is within well-organized support groups. A healthy support group has good leadership that understands the balance of grace and truth. One cannot be present without the other. These might include formal therapy groups, twelve-step programs, prayer groups, or groups that form around a common challenge, like sexual addiction or abuse recovery.[62]

Therapy is another refuge. I have had great therapists and terrible therapists, so I understand how hard it can be to find someone with whom you connect. Therapy can be an invaluable resource, and I cannot recommend it enough. The opportunity to share with someone who is legally obligated to confidentiality and who focuses solely on you and your needs is truly a gift!

Finally and most importantly, God yearns for you to draw near to him. Experience the freedom of his light and be set free!

Bring It to Life

- Read Luke 7:36–50. This is a beautiful account of a woman who yearned for the light. What do you notice about her, about Jesus, and the Pharisee? Imagine that if she represents you, then Jesus is the safe person, and the Pharisee is the unsafe person.

- Be aware of light around you, whether candles or stars or the warmth of the sun. Let it remind you of the power of light and the ways we are drawn toward it.

- Write down the names of the people closest to you. Do you feel they illustrate characteristics of someone who is safe or unsafe?

- If you find yourself surrounded by unsafe people, I recommend the book *Safe People* by Dr. Henry Cloud and Dr. John Townsend.

Jesus, the Word and the Light, I pray I will step into the freedom of your grace and truth. I pray that I will find those people who are safe, who are human representations of who you are. Lord, thank you for being so vulnerable, for showing me all the thoughts and qualities that make up who you are. May I continue to know you more and more through your Word and feel more and more whole in the warmth of your light.

DAY 25

Fire

GENESIS 15:5–21; EXODUS 3:1–21;
1 KINGS 18:20–39; ACTS 2:1–4

Fire fell from the sky in 1 Kings 13 and burned up the offering on the altar in such a grand display that it destroyed everything. What an incredible experience for everyone present! And how terrifying!

It was not the only time God manifested himself in the form of fire. The account in Genesis 15 of God passing as a torch between the dead animals might seem confusing, but in the ancient world, it was customary to make a legal contract. Typically, the parties cut the animals in half and divided the meat between them, with the understanding that if one party did not abide by the agreement, they would be like the dead animals around them.[63] However, it is curious that this covenant only goes one way: God is the only One who makes a promise. Abraham has only to receive it. It was the promise to provide an heir and protect his descendants, symbolized as God "walked" as a flame through the dead animals that night.

Centuries later, when it was time to fulfill the first instance of protecting Abraham's descendants, God chose to appear as fire once again. This time, he appeared to Moses in a burning bush. It was as if God was showing that he had not changed.

God kept his promise and rescued Abraham's descendants from Egypt. For forty years, God appeared as a flame every night, leading them through the desert. He faithfully transformed himself into a burning torch that lit up the night sky. I have often imagined how comforting it would be to see God, as a fiery torch, camped outside of my home.

Jesus came to the earth centuries later for another rescue mission. But this time it was to rescue all people. The goal was to free all of humanity from spiritual slavery—forever. After Jesus successfully defeated death and rose from the dead, the Holy Spirit arrived on Pentecost in the form of a flame, as if to remind us again that he had not changed. He was the same God who had promised deliverance all those years ago.

Why might God choose fire? Fire is powerful, comforting, useful, and essential. Fire is a source of light and a source of heat. The sound of a crackling fire can be soothing. A fire can be a place of meeting, where people commune with each other. Fire also has the potential to be dangerous. It can be turned into a weapon that destroys, kills, and terrorizes. In the wild, this destructive quality is useful since it's an essential part of the growth process in forests and jungles. Fire burns out old growth and makes room for new growth. What a beautiful representation of the various dimensions of our God.

A key element to all four of these Bible stories is that the flame of God was not fueled by anything other than himself. Even in the account where he appeared to Moses in a burning bush, the bush did not burn up. God is self-reliant and self-sustaining, and he creates energy by his own power.

You are not meant to create your own fire; you are meant to rely on the God who has more than enough energy and stamina to keep you going. The beauty of the fire he builds inside of you is that he will sustain it, and it will remain unchanged.

As I was contemplating this book, I hiked to Bridal Veil Falls in Dupont State Park. As I sat at the falls, I felt God prompting me, telling me that yes, I was to write this book, but it would be difficult. And he wanted me to be sure to let him do the work, not me. I agreed, and again I felt him urging me to remember that he would do it, not me. I returned from my hike feeling excited. I had a plan, and without realizing it, I stopped praying to him, too busy with my own vision of what to do. I came up with an outline, had my timeline in place, and began working. All the while, I kept telling myself I would let God do it through me.

I assumed that when he told me it would be difficult, he meant that the writing would be difficult. What I did not anticipate is that the writing would not be the hard part; it was circumstances around me that would make it hard. So many things happened shortly after I began writing. We received my dad's cancer diagnosis and experienced new challenges at church. The world around us became increasingly unstable, and I fell ill.

One night, as I was lying in bed sick, I became upset with God. I accused him of not giving me enough information before agreeing to do this project. He and I both knew that, had I realized the things about to happen, I would not have put myself in a position where I felt a project would be so impossible to finish. Even in my agreement with God that day at the falls, I was still so stubborn in relying on myself and not him. I had lied to myself because deep down, I believed I could do it myself. It is a tough habit to break, even when I am as weak a person as I am. And so, like an angry child, I made my point known.

In his kindness, he drew me close to him, like two friends who meet by a campfire for a private moment. He whispered, *Remember, you are not able to do this. I am going to do this.* I was panicking because I had made a dangerous assumption. I had lived under the belief that God only gives us what we can handle. That is a lie. God will absolutely give you more than you can handle, and then he will step in and do the unthinkable through you. You are not capable of building a fire that never dies or one that is so impressive that it falls from the sky, burning up everything in its path.

The creativity of coming to us in the form of a flame is that he can vary his approach to us based on our needs. In my frustration and anger, he came to me like a campfire, the relational God who welcomes me for a conversation. When I fear my enemy, Satan, God comes like a raging fire, placing himself between me and my enemy. When I feel lost, he comes like a burning torch, leading the way on a dark night.

I know times will come when the idea of God providing this variety of help seems far-fetched. But get on your knees, press into him, and tell him that you need him. I can make you two promises: The first is that you will be given more than you can handle even if it isn't presently happening in your life. The second promise is that when you find yourself in that moment, stop and decipher which dimension of God, which element of fire you need most. Pursue him and ask others for help. God will do incredible things in and through you.

Bring It to Life

· Analyze your heart and God's character based on the different dimensions of fire. How does your life relate to God in each of these areas?

> ➤ Light (giving direction)

> ➤ Comfort (offering relationship)

> ➤ Protection (providing safety)

> ➤ Removal of garbage (forgiving sin)

> ➤ Making way for new growth (pushing you to grow)

· Is there one (or more) of the aforementioned areas in which you struggle? Which one, and why?

· Each time you encounter fire, meditate on the Lord and the elements of who he is. What do you notice?

All powerful God, thank you for using fire to show me the dimensions of who you are. Thank you that you are kind, all-knowing, powerful, dangerous, surprising, and unchanging. I pray I will acknowledge my continual need for you daily. I pray I will never assume that I can do anything on my own. I rely on your help, your inspiration, and your care. Please work mightily in and through me for your glory.

The Rock

Psalm 18:1–3; Psalm 19:7–14; Psalm 92;
Isaiah 26:2–12; Matthew 7:24–27

One night many years ago, I was reading through a workbook on anxiety and began to reflect on some of my journals and notes. I decided to try a little exercise of my own to sort out what was at the heart of my anxiety in order to uncover my greatest fear. I concluded it was loss, specifically the idea of having something or someone I love or care about taken away from me.

I wrote down things that I thought would be difficult to lose but also felt confident that I could handle well enough. I made note that this list contained only physical things: my car, my house, and my belongings. Then I started to write the names of people who are dear to me. I thought about my friends and determined it would be painful to lose any of them, but I believed I would be able to find the strength to manage such a loss.

I worked my way toward my inner circle, my family. The idea of losing my parents was devastating, but I could also imagine God's peace. I thought of my husband and how traumatizing it would be to lose him. Because of Tim's medical condition, I had already been working through the possibility of losing him and felt more assured that God would sustain me.

Finally, I came to the last person on my list: my son, Carter. He was my only child at that time. Anxiety pulsated through my core as I stared at his name. Without thought or hesitation, I said to God, *No. You can take anything else from me. But you cannot take him. I would not survive.*

In a rush of grace and compassion, I felt God reply, *I understand how hard that would be. It is the price I paid for you.* Suddenly, the most famous Bible verse of my childhood had new meaning: "For God so loved the world, that He gave His only Son, that whoever believes in him should not perish but have eternal life" (John 3:16 ESV). His only Son. It was in that moment that I recognized the pure strength and might of God and his commitment to me.

He is called "the Rock" on more than one occasion, and the imagery and metaphor of this word evoke an image of a solid foundation. In Psalm 18:2, the writer uses two different words that mean "rock," as if to encompass all possible meanings. [64] When paired with God, the word *rock* has many implications; he is a fortress of protection, dependable, and steadfast. [65]

At the beginning of today's devotion, we read passages from Psalms 19 and 92 and Isaiah 26 in which the word *rock* appears and can mean a refuge made from a "cliff or large rock." [66] The imagery was that of a fortress set up high on a solid foundation. Jesus applied this picture to our lives: the Rock represents his words. God and his words are the fortress that protect our spirits. God and his words are the only things that do not change. Everything else has the potential to be different tomorrow.

My anxiety is the fear that something terrible will happen, and I will not be prepared or able to survive the experience. I used to spend a lot of time reasoning that the worst will not happen, but I have found that true and lasting peace comes from the idea that because of God, I can withstand anything. It is not that I am strong and capable to handle life on my own. Goodness, no. But in the moment when God revealed to me the depth of his sacrifice by giving his Son, I realized just how powerful it is to have his Spirit residing in me. If God can withstand such as loss, then surely he can give me the supernatural strength to survive any dangers in this world.

It was also illuminating to realize that my anxiety stemmed from the false belief that I could somehow hold on to everything. Instead, I had to recognize that the world around us is temporary and always shifting. It is in a perpetual state of change, and the things we hold on to today will one day be gone, even things that seem perfectly stable. Possessions are lost, broken, repossessed, destroyed by a natural disaster, stolen, or sold. People fade away whether through distance, discord, disease, or death. But one thing never changes, and that is God and his Word. I used to be terrified of losing the temporary but have grown more and more in love with God's permanence. The key is to stay safe in his fortress.

The world will try to entice you out of the place that offers the most security and peace. The culture around us seems focused on avoiding pain at all costs and, if in pain, using distractions and pleasure to cope. Many alternative, attractive philosophies also exist, and their ideas may sound good. However, the strength found in God is that he gives purpose to all pain, making it possible to push through.

In Psalm 18, the Hebrew word for "rock" is a bit different. It is a word that refers more to a hiding place, a refuge, that offers a different kind of protection.[67] Not only does God want to provide a large stronghold for you, but he also creates personal hiding places to protect you. For me, the hardest part of staying safely in his fortress or in the craggy rock of his hiding place is that it is difficult to see the world through spiritual eyes and not just physical eyes. In order to capture this security, it is essential to reframe the world from the Lord's perspective.

This new way of looking at the world has revolutionized how I pray. Because of my dad's cancer treatments, people continually tell me that they are praying for our family. Years ago, I would have focused all my prayers on asking God to keep my dad safe and to fight the cancer for us. But I am no longer trapped by those fears. I still ask God to make the treatments successful, but my prayers have transitioned in the sense that I am also able to admit that I do not know the best plan for my life or my dad's, and if it is God's will to have my dad die, then I pray that I will see all of the beauty in the time I have left with him. The fear of loss has become the freedom of possibility.

I still wrestle with the fear of losing Carter and now Matthew. When I talk with people who have lost a child or see someone on the news discuss a missing child, my heart flips upside down. It is still at the heart of my worst fears. As I walk more and more with God, I become more convinced that even if someday I should lose one of my sons, I will be able to find spiritual safety and security in the comforts of his promises and his character. God loves me, wants good things for me, and will never fail me. He is the same yesterday, today, and forever!

Bring It to Life

· What is your greatest fear? What power has it had over you? How has it influenced you?

· Imagine a fortress sitting high on a cliff (maybe even draw it in your journal). Mentally place yourself in that fortress. What promises of God hold you there? I encourage you to go on a journey through the Bible to find attributes of God and imagine building up your fortress walls with those words.

God, our Rock, our Fortress, our Hiding Place, you go by all of those names. I pray you will give me a spiritual eye to see the world in the way you see it. Lord, I pray that fear will not hold power in my life but instead see the world as you see it. Give me the ability to live freely from the worries of what I might lose and embrace all that I gain from having you as my God. You are unchanging.

High Priest

LUKE 23:20–49; 1 PETER 2:4–12;
HEBREWS 6:19–20; 4:14–5:9

In the aftermath of my psychiatric hospitalization, I felt embarrassed, frustrated with myself, and afraid to go out in public. I remember trying to go to church, but my impression of myself had changed. I was twenty-one and believed my future was bleak. I couldn't imagine doing ministry full-time since I had a suicide attempt in my history. And after a hospitalization, it is difficult to hide from the truth about yourself. I felt like my suicide attempt was now tied to my identity.

I walked in the woods close to our home to sit with God and discuss my frustration and insecurity. I felt discounted and less valuable than other believers, and I was tired of being weak. Having to watch Tim deal with the pressure from our church leadership to find a fix for me only fueled my belief that our days in ministry were numbered, all thanks to me.

I heard other believers talk about their love for God, and I listened as they shared beautiful stories of answered prayers in their lives. It made me feel jealous and hurt. Why was my story such a disaster? I felt my presence in the Christian community held no value, that I was a "less than" believer. But years later, something clicked that transformed my perspective of who I am.

To capture this, first go back to the story of Jesus' death. He was on the cross, and the whole world suddenly became dark because the sun stopped shining. After hours of pain and agony, Jesus announced that he was ready to die and gave up his spirit. At that moment, in the temple, the sound of fabric tearing could be heard as the massive curtain that separated the people from the presence of God was torn from top to bottom (Mark 15:38).

In Exodus, God created a system for the Israelites to use so that they could be in relationship with him. Because of God's holiness, humans could not be in his full presence without instantly dying. Therefore, God designed a room called the "Holy of Holies" (Exodus 26:33 AMP), which only the high priest could enter once a year in order to burn incense and offer sacrifices to God on behalf of the people (Leviticus 16). A massive wall of curtains was constructed per the Lord's instructions to separate his holy dwelling place from the people. The curtain guarding the Holy of Holies was actually eleven curtains put together. According to Exodus 26, the curtains totaled thirty cubits long and four cubits wide, which equated to over fifty feet tall and seven feet thick.

Imagine the shock when the curtain separating God from humans was torn by God himself. It was a physical demonstration that a barrier no longer separated God from his people. Now everyone was welcome to enter the presence of God without fear. The moment of Jesus' death changed the spiritual world for eternity.

I can't imagine how Satan and his demonic forces responded. God had promised at the beginning of creation that he would have victory in the fight against Satan for human salvation. So many things in the Old Testament prophesied the coming of Jesus. Now, in Jesus' death, he brought a permanent gateway to peace with God. Sin and death no longer had a hold on humankind!

Because of Jesus' sacrifice, God gave him the title of High Priest, and he holds that title for all eternity. He stands before the Father and advocates on our behalf. As with the human high priests through history, Jesus also bears the responsibility of overseeing all other priests. The question becomes who now holds the position of priest? You do.

You, as a follower of Jesus, now have the sacred role of joining what Peter called the "royal priesthood" (1 Peter 2:9). Do not confuse this title with the Old Testament role of a priest. You are not being called to offer physical sacrifices or perform spiritual rites, but you are now representing God to the world.[68]

I have had Christian clients who, instead of feeling like a priest, have felt as I did: that they were lacking spiritually, and other Christians appeared more qualified. But the truth is that your qualifications were given to you the moment you chose to be a follower of Jesus, and the title of priest is a part of who you are. It is now part of your spiritual DNA.

The need for your contribution to the cause of Jesus cannot be understated. Your everyday ministry might not include the same sacramental duties of an Old Testament priest, but the nature of their duties has been transformed into things you do on a daily basis. Your prayers are like the incense burned before God (Psalm 141:2). I imagine the voices of all of God's priests praying to him fill his throne room with a wonderful aroma. Even when your prayers involve anger, hurt, and frustration, they have value because your words are working out your relationship to God. And in place of animal sacrifice, God's true desire is to have fellowship with you. Psalm 51:17 beautifully displays this truth: "The sacrifices of God are a broken spirit; a broken and contrite heart, O God, you will not despise" (ESV).

The twisted beauty of a broken heart is that it is a sacred gift to God. On that day in the woods, when I approached him with nothing to show but brokenness, his affections for my gift overflowed. I still have times when I struggle with this truth. I want to come before him with an offering of the number of people I have inspired or the good things I have accomplished for the day, but his idea of a beautiful gift is my humble spirit.

The other powerful application of your position as a priest is that you have gained direct access to God. Whether you serve as a pastor of a church or as someone working in the world of business, the value of your ministry and work is essential. Jesus is our High Priest, and those of us who are his followers share in his work (1 Peter 2: 4–12).

Maybe your priestly duties involve attending to your responsibilities each day, as Jesus did for thirty years, and inter-acting with coworkers, family, and friends in a manner that pays honor to God. By being present, you bring Jesus' influence and presence into your conversations and interactions with people. God is sending you out, as his mediator, to reach the people around you. When you pray for others, you are the mediator bringing people before him. He is always actively engaged and attentive to your conversations with him.

Jesus taught that humble prayers, offered in secret and with simple words, are treasured and valued by God (Luke 18:9–14; Matthew 6:5–8). You are truly a treasured piece in God's priest-hood. Never doubt that!

BRING IT TO LIFE

· Get a piece of cloth, close your eyes, and rip it half. Let the sound remind you of the beautiful moment when God tore open the barriers between you and him.

· Think of things you naturally enjoy and how you could incorporate those into your priestly duties. For example, I love horseback riding and joined a group with whom I can ride, listen, and minister to. They bless me too!

· Watch your thoughts this week and see if you compare yourself to other believers or feel "less than" because of your role. Journal your thoughts about yourself and make note of any comparisons you're making to others. Those comparisons do not hold truth!

Jesus, my High Priest, who daily represents me before God and has mercy and compassion for me, I pray you will open my eyes to the ways you are working in and through me. Give me a vision of how you are using me as a priest in my daily life and how my gifts and talents can continually bring your hope and message to those around me. May I see myself as you see me: a beautiful priest in the service of my High Priest, the One who made a way for my relationship with you!

Exorcist

LUKE 8:26–38; MARK 7:24–30;
LUKE 4:1–12; MATTHEW 16:21–28

Back in 2002, I participated in a Dialectical Behavioral Therapy group and was doing well. My employer graciously allowed me to take time twice a week to attend the group to work through my depression. Although I had not been suicidal or required hospitalization, I still battled a roller coaster of emotions. I enjoyed days of clarity and joy but also days of darkness, lethargy, and sadness. Nevertheless, I felt as though I was finally breaking free.

I returned home before Tim one night and was unloading the dishwasher when I found myself holding a knife. I stopped to look at it and felt a sudden urge to hold it even longer. Then a rush of thoughts came in like flood: *You can't keep fighting. You are tired and worn out, and you will never be well. This knife is the key to your freedom. You could be in eternity with Jesus tonight. You have a choice.*

Unlike my previous experiences, this one was different. I immediately recognized that this voice was not mine. The thoughts, however, still confused me. The truths were twisted and tightly bound with lies. I *did* have a choice. I could give up and go to heaven that night. I *was* tired of fighting and exhausted from a long week. But I heard the lie in the words, "You will never be well." Something rustled within me; those words just did not sound right. Torn, I tried to sort through it in my mind and determine whether that statement was true. I couldn't be sure.

Thankfully, Tim came home and interrupted my chain of thoughts. He chatted about his day, asked questions, and talked about what we should do for dinner. Meanwhile the voice persisted, sounding confident and accusatory. I wanted to finish my internal dialogue, so I told Tim I needed to use the bathroom. I tucked the knife against me and snuck upstairs, locking the bathroom door behind me. I needed time and space to decide for myself.

Tim noticed and was at the door of the bathroom, demanding I open it. I started to cry and begged him to give me a minute to think, but he was insistent. He told me to open the door, or he would knock it down. I unlocked it, and he rushed in. He hugged me and asked what had happened, so I shared my internal dialogue with him and how it had played out.

We contemplated the situation and came to a conclusion: Satan did not want me to get well. In a moment when I was tired and alone, Satan took the opportunity to brew a concoction of truths and lies and feed it to me in the hopes that I would act this time. Although it was a terrifying thought, there was also power in the realization that I had the Holy Spirit working to combat the lies, and the more time I spent studying the Bible, the more clearly I could discern lies from truth. The Bible is called a sword (Ephesians 6:17) and for a good reason.

The tricky part of the battle we face with Satan is that he also knows the Bible, as evidenced by his conversation with Jesus in the desert (Matthew 4:1–11). He does not seem to show any fear of Jesus in their recorded interactions, unlike other demonic characters. Did you notice in the other Scripture passages how the demons screamed, begged for mercy, and were even forced to give up their victims whether Jesus was physically present or not? Satan, however, appears to be much more manipulative, self-controlled, and clever. He works to appeal to the nature of the listener, mixing truth with lies and presenting it in a seemingly reasonable manner.

To make it additionally confusing, Satan can use other believers to deliver his message. As you read in Luke, Peter's protest to Jesus' death seems like a rational sentiment or at least a harmless statement. But Jesus identifies the true source of the thought: Satan. Satan can use the well-meaning words of other believers to steer you in the wrong direction. I myself had a "Peter moment" in which I meant to speak truth, but my human logic was not promoting what Jesus taught. It was in a conversation with my oldest son, Carter.

Carter is incredibly spiritually perceptive. Even from a young age, he had a deep desire to know and follow Jesus. I remember when we first told Carter about communion. He was around seven years old, and we explained that the bread was the reminder of Jesus' broken body, and the juice or wine represented his shed blood. When the plate came by, Carter took a whole handful of bread, for which I scolded him. He turned to me in confusion and whispered, "But Mom, if this is Jesus, why wouldn't you take as much of him as you can?"

One night, we were discussing with Carter the transition that comes with a new brother. I was giving him advice with an air of confidence from my expertise as a therapist. After listening to my advice, Carter looked puzzled and said, "I am trying to live by what the Bible is calling me to do. To be patient, humble, and kind." It was in that moment that I realized my worldly wisdom and feedback had created confusion for my son, who was trying to submit to God. What an incredibly humbling moment!

God's truth opens our eyes to Satan's mind games. The beauty of my experience in talking with Carter is that I was misguided, but he held fast to the truth. And by sharing that truth with me, I was able to recenter myself. We are not only meant to learn the Word but to also assist each other.

If you are a follower of Jesus, know that Satan does not want you alive and active. You are a threat to his cause, and the more spiritual depth you gain, the more dangerous you become. The Bible is your weapon, your tool to identify and reject his lies. Satan and his demons have no authority over Jesus, so learn Jesus' words and use them against him. We do not need to be afraid. Each and every story in which Jesus encounters Satan and his demons, Jesus demonstrates his authority.

As I held the knife in my hand that night, a haunting voice whispered lies to me. I have gotten stronger, not on my own will power but with the power of his Word coupled with tools he has provided, such as therapy, community, and medication. Now I move offensively against Satan by sharing my testimony. You can do this too!

I don't know what motivated you to pick up this book, but let this be the moment when you are assured that the words "you will never get better" embody a lie straight from the pit of hell. You may struggle your whole life, but struggle and defeat are not the same. You serve a God who makes demons shudder. He already defeated Satan. Stay in the fight!

Bring It to Life

- Regularly study the Bible both independently and in groups. Books, YouTube videos, and online Bible study courses can help guide your personal studies. For studying in a group setting, join a Bible study through a church, an organization, or a gathering of other believers.

- Write out your thoughts today and track them to identify any patterns. If a thought enters your mind that encourages self-harm or suicide, remember that it is a lie. What emotions do those thoughts evoke? Once you identify the emotion, research that emotion in the Bible and find verses that address it directly. If this feels overwhelming, ask a pastor or friend to assist you. This is one way of responding to your fears and emotions with the authority of Jesus, who lives in you.

- Remain connected to other believers who are ready and willing to support you. If you're experiencing recurring suicidal thoughts or self-harm, see a counselor. Group therapy can also be helpful.

Lord God, the One who crushes Satan's lies and brings freedom with truth, I pray that you will be the One whom I hear and turn to when life gets hard. If suicidal ideation or thoughts come, I pray you will drive them out with your truth, that Satan's lies will be obvious and easy to recognize. May the Word come to life as I study it. May I continually learn how to use your words as my defense against our enemy.

Mother Hen

MATTHEW 23:37; PSALM 17:7–8; PSALM 91

My husband, Tim, grew up in the mountains of North Carolina. As a kid, he and his family cared for a variety of animals, including two species of chickens: Rhode Island Reds and Bantams. I asked him what mother hens are like when protecting their chicks, and he explained that mother hens are extremely attentive and protective. Tim said on one occasion, he watched one of his hens chase a large great horned owl, swatting at the owl's eyes in an effort to blind the predator.

Hens have a brilliant way of suddenly making their chicks "disappear" by hiding them under their wings. I have no personal experience with chickens, so I went online and watched video after video of mother hens gathering their young and tucking them safely under their wings. Predators circling in the skies or stalking them on the ground can no longer find the defenseless babies; they literally disappear out of sight.

Chicks cannot detect if danger is near, and they lack defense mechanisms of their own. Instead, they obediently follow their mother and hide upon her direction. Chicks even begin communicating with their mother before they hatch.[69] In picturing all those little chicks safely huddled under their mother's wings, I imagine they have no real concept of the potential dangers of the world. Within the safety of her protective wings, they rest.

Jesus uses the analogy of hens when describing his yearning to provide the same kind of attention, love, and protection to his people that hens provide their chicks. With words like *refuge* and *shield*, Psalm 91 draws hard-hitting parallels to God's mothering feathers. What Jesus' listeners did not understand was that he also wept over the impending destruction of Jerusalem, the very city in which they stood, which would occur shortly after his death.

He had sent prophets and teachers to warn his people of their spiritual danger, and not only did they kill the messengers, but they also killed Jesus, who had explained earlier that the killings would continue until his return as King. Sure enough, in AD 70, a Jewish revolt against the Roman empire resulted in military measures and brutal retaliation. The Romans, led by a man named Titus, destroyed the city and the temple.[70]

Jesus wants to be the safe place we can run to when we're overwhelmed by the world. Imagine God sweeping you under the shelter of his wings, where you don't have to anticipate danger and where predators cannot find you. Remember, Satan is the enemy, and the Bible says he is actively hunting you (1 Peter 5:8).

My greatest experience of God's sheltering happened in the fall of 2004. Tim and I had dinner plans to celebrate my birthday with friends. At the time, I was three months pregnant, we had recently bought a house, and everything seemed perfect. Tim had been having recurring headaches, so we decided to stop at urgent care before heading to the restaurant.

When we arrived at the emergency room, the doctor listened to Tim's symptoms and suggested the headaches were stress related. But Tim was adamant that something was wrong, so the doctor agreed to order a CAT scan. I sat in the waiting room, and the doctor didn't return for a long time. When he did, he was accompanied by another physician. Together they explained that Tim was in an ambulance and on his way to a much larger hospital, where I was to meet him and they would explain everything. I remember crying, driving to the hospital, finding Tim in the ICU, and meeting with specialists to discuss emergency brain surgery for the following day.

Interestingly, the part that stands out in my memory was leaving the hospital alone, without Tim. My mind and emotions hadn't caught up with the reality of what was taking place. I was still dressed nicely for dinner. Life had blindsided me.

My parents offered to let me sleep at their place since their house was closer to the hospital than ours. I cried like a child that night, begging God not to leave me. I felt overwhelmed with all the implications of Tim's brain surgery and the risks involved. I tried to figure out how I would be a strong wife, a soon-to-be mom, and still work my job as we navigated this new medical challenge. It was too much.

I'm not sure at what hour it happened, but I do remember falling asleep. It was not that I had suddenly stumbled upon the solutions for all my questions or that I had some guarantees that things would be fine. It was a feeling of confidence that I could be at peace under the shelter of the mighty wings of my God even though chaos had upended my world.

My God is the One who walked through the fiery furnace with Shadrach, Meshach, and Abednego (Daniel 3:23–28). He is the One who climbed into the lions' den to save Daniel (Daniel 6:13–24). He walked on water with Peter (Matthew 14:28–31), and he took down Goliath with his young warrior, David (1 Samuel 17). My God is not a bystander; he is always active and present.

My body, mind, and heart had been robbed of all strength, and I could practically feel God physically wrap me up and hide me away. Everything quieted, and I fell asleep. Like a mother hen, my Lord gathered up his chick and secured her safely under his wing, rocking me to sleep and reminding me that he would protect me through the night while I rested.

I do not know what perils you are facing or have faced. Sometimes it's the pain of the monotony, the emotional toil of dealing with the same struggles day in and day out that are upsetting. Sometimes it is the horrible agony of one moment in time that changed our lives forever in a way that cannot be undone. Regardless of the type of pain you face, let our great and mighty God tuck you away safely. Stop wrestling, planning, and problem-solving for a moment and fall into the hiding place of his name. If your body, mind, and emotions are spent, then take time to sit and simply be with him.

· Go online and watch videos of hens gathering their chicks under them. It is a perfect, beautiful illustration of how God wants to protect us from the world.

· Draw an image of you and put a semicircle around it, marking it as God's protective nature. What things do you feel are "hunting" you right now? Is it the pressures of the world? A tough situation? Daily stressors? Write those outside of the semicircle.

· Allow God to gather you close to him. Sometimes when I climb into bed and pull up the covers, I imagine his covering is much like the blanket and keeping me safe and warm. Use your imagination to picture God wrapping around you his incredible power, the power that has accomplished amazing things throughout the ages.

My dearest Jesus, please tuck me under your wing today and every day. I know that life is hard sometimes and seems to be on repeat. The sameness can strain me. Life can also become challenging in the blink of an eye, leaving me bewildered and forever changed. Whether I face daily hardships or struggle with new challenges, I pray that I will gather close to you and allow your covering to keep me safe from the terrors and troubles of this world. Thank you for doing life with me.

Genesis 8:6–11; Matthew 3:13–17; Romans 5:1–11

It is not a coincidence that I have chosen two birds, back-to-back, to represent two different aspects of God. As Jesus used the metaphor of the mother hen to describe his protective nature over us, the Bible describes the Spirit as a dove, showcasing a different aspect of the Deity.

A dove appears in the of harrowing tale of Noah and the flood. In Genesis, we read the account of the flood and how God provided Noah with the schematics to help him build an enormous boat. It was essentially a floating zoo that would carry him, his family, and members of the animal kingdom through the most devastating natural disaster of all time. To make matters worse, Noah had no clue as to how long he and his family would remain on the ark. I cannot imagine being stranded on a boat for months with no end in sight. After months and months of waiting, Noah released a dove to go forth and bring back a sign of nearby land. As you read in Genesis, the dove returned to the ark with no such indication. On the second attempt, Noah's feathered friend brought back evidence that the earth was regenerating: an olive branch!

The dove had chosen a symbolic item; it was a promise. Noah could not have known it at the time, but the Spirit delivered a symbol that God weaves throughout the redemption story. The olive branch became a symbol of peace for all time and an image that God would use as one of his trademarks.

After the flood, God instructed the Israelites on the importance of anointing oil, which would be used for kings. One required ingredient was olive oil (Exodus 30:22–25). When Jesus lived in Jerusalem, he spent a considerable amount of time at the Mount of Olives. Most notably, Jesus prayed his most vulnerable and heart-wrenching prayer to the Father at the Mount of Olivers, where he was arrested (Luke 22:39–54). After Jesus' death, Paul described God's people in terms of olive branches (Romans 11:13–22). Even down to Revelation, God uses olive trees in his imagery to depict godly people standing before the Lord (Revelation 11:4). God has a fascinating way of carefully depositing his signature throughout the story of the Bible to show that he is intimately involved with us. Things that seem like coincidences are in fact orchestrations of his genius.

Although the dove is an international symbol for peace, the dove also embodies hope, particularly in the story of the flood. Imagine the celebration that must have taken place when Noah and his family received physical evidence that their hope of one day disembarking from the ark and starting a new life would come true. What incredible news!

Studies have shown that hope is directly linked with stronger mental health in the wake of such a disaster.[71] Hope equates to a kind of optimism that certain things will happen. In the unpredictable world we live in, it can be difficult to know what we can and cannot put our hope in. God answers that question for us. Paul's words in Romans tell us that suffering can drive us to hope because it strengthens our understanding of Jesus, who suffered on our behalf. We have hope because Jesus was willing to be tortured and killed for people who hated him, and he will not leave his followers without an eternal future full of goodness.

For me, the toughest part of hope is that it requires a spiritual eye, one that looks beyond the physical world around us. I feel like I am living on the ark; every day in this world, I have the deep sense that I am not home yet. I have not reached my destination. But the beauty of the Spirit delivering figurative olive leaves to me is the refreshment my soul needs. He delivers them to me in the forms of promises in the Bible, encouragement from my fellow brothers and sisters, and blessings God gives me each day.

God is weaving your story, and if you watch closely, you will find elements that appear to be coincidences that actually make up the moving parts of your life. Things will sometimes seem to be products of chance, but in truth, you will look back and see the mark of his work. Depression will work hard to hide the olive leaves that God delivers to you. It will take you to the deck of your ark, where it will point at the deep water and the dark, looming skies to convince you that all is hopeless. But God promises that good things are ahead. He also wants to illuminate the gifts he continues to provide in the present.

I have experienced so many random coincidences in my life that I later realized were reminders from the Spirit of things I had already learned or seen. The most powerful example in my life happened in 2016. I flew to Minneapolis after receiving a call from my dad that my mom had Guillain-Barré and was moved to the intensive care unit at Abbot Northwestern Hospital. My dad picked me up from the airport, and we drove straight to the hospital. As we parked, I realized this was the same unit where Tim had been taken the night before his brain surgery all those years ago. I crossed familiar hallways, and when we reached the ICU, I took a deep breath. Even years later, the waiting room looked the same to me.

What truly caught me off guard was that my mom's room was in the same cluster of rooms where Tim had been. Suddenly, it was as if a voice whispered, *I was here with you thirteen years ago; I am here still. I knew this day was coming. Trust me.* I felt a calming peace. Despite the unknown that lay ahead, God had designed a scenario in which I was physically reminded of his care for me. He began flooding my mind with various Bible passages that speak of God's strength and love. Scripture was coming alive right in front of me as the Spirit repeatedly told me that I was not alone. There was hope!

Hope is not the only thing that the Spirit offers in the form of a dove. The dove also represents innocence (Matthew 10:16). Doves were used as sacrifices after babies' births (Leviticus 12:6–7), or the poor could substitute a dove in the place of a lamb as a way to make peace with God (Leviticus 5:7). God is continually working to rescue you and provide you with enduring peace and hope.

As you read the story of Jesus' baptism, when he came up from the water and the dove descended, it was as if the Spirit said, "Here he is! The hope of Noah is yours and will continue on!"

Bring It to Life

- Carefully consider the twists and turns of your life. Do you notice any coincidences that were actually huge turning points in your life? Journal about these coincidences and share them with someone.

- Keep an eye out for the olive branches that God extends to us through the Bible. Stay close to the Word and continually feed hope to keep you going.

- Let the image of a dove remind you that the Spirit is constantly working, continually carrying a message through your life. Find hope in it.

Lord God, thank you for being so intimately involved in my life that you are creating a story that brings your words to life. Jesus, I am grateful for your sacrifice, and I pray I will have my spiritual eyes opened to see you working in and around me. Give me the spiritual wisdom to see the good things you are doing and to take note of the divine coincidences that lead us toward what is good. Thank you for continually providing us with new hope.

The Family

GENESIS 1:26–27; LUKE 3:21–22;
JOHN 14:23–31; GALATIANS 3:26–4:7

I truly believe that God wanted this name saved for the end of our time together because it captures the heart and soul of the triune God: the Father, the Son, and the Spirit. The human concept of family is not something that God models himself after; rather, he modeled the human concept of family after him. The family God designed was not intended for harm but for good. Sadly, as sinners, our experience of family is not always a positive or healthy one. If you have been or are currently in a family that has been harmful to you, then my hope is that your heavenly family will bring healing to you.

God's triune nature as one God in three persons displays relationship within the unity of God, and we, too, were created for interpersonal relationships. We can learn so much about the concept of family by reflecting on how the three persons of the Trinity interact and support each other. The Father designed the plan, the Son (Jesus) secured the plan, and the Spirit is the helper, who offers support and guidance as he applies the plan to our lives.

The God of heaven—the Father, the Son, and the Spirit—all wanted you. At the heart of this plan, which centered around self-sacrifice, was love for you. They dreamed of adopting you into the family, and each person of the Trinity took on different roles to bring their plan to fruition.

I had the beautiful opportunity to experience this dream as a child. When I was eleven years old, my parents told my brother, Jon, and me that they wanted to adopt a baby from Korea. We were ecstatic and joined our parents in the process of bringing a child into our family, which meant a lot of paperwork and interviews. As the process unfolded, we received a polaroid picture in the mail of a baby boy in the arms of the woman who was fostering him. We put it on the fridge and dreamed of the day he would join us. We even held a family meeting to discuss the name of our newest family member. After much debate and discussion, his name was chosen: Karl James Watje. All of us helped assemble his crib in my parents' bedroom, and we chose a teddy-bear theme for his bedding and blankets. Jon and I picked out toys that we thought he would like, and we waited in anticipation.

I vividly recall the day Karl arrived. The adoption agency shared the details of his arrival, and we all dressed up out of sheer excitement before heading to the airport. We installed the car seat, drove to the airport, and waited at his arrival gate. All the passengers deplaned, and we stood among two other families who waited for their adopted babies. Suddenly, all three babies arrived in the terminal in the arms of chaperones who had traveled with them from Korea.

Our six-month-old little boy, wide-eyed and beautiful, was dressed in the sweetest blue outfit. My parents scooped him up, and then we sat on the floor of the terminal to admire him. He was precious, just like his picture! We carried him to the car and drove home, where all our friends from the neighborhood gathered to meet him. The next day, my parents brought the baby to my class for show-and-tell at school. It was a time of celebration!

If this is how a human family experiences adoption, then I cannot imagine the thrill and commitment that the Father, the Son, and the Spirit feel about adopting you—the child they not only love but also created. How thrilling it is when you choose to be adopted and experience God's gift of salvation by placing your faith in Jesus, the Son. And when we get to heaven, we receive a new name (Revelation 2:17). How beautiful is that?

We truly cannot comprehend the celebration and excitement on the day we finally arrive home. The dream of a forever family will have finally come to fruition. But until we arrive at our final home, the Spirit is here to coach, counsel, and help us, just as he helped Jesus, who stands in the presence of the Father and continually advocates for us with compassion, kindness, and unconditional love.

The Father also has a special relationship with you. In Romans 8:14–17, Paul wrote that through our adoption, we get to call him "Abba, Father," which has a special meaning. The term *Abba* is an affectionate term for Father, a name that would indicate emotional closeness.[72] Jesus told a story in Luke 15:11–31 that was meant to show the depth of love of the Father. In his story, Jesus described a family in which the father was generous and kind, giving his youngest son his inheritance early and watching him leave for a life of recklessness and foolishness. The son made terrible choices and lived so scandalously that he lost his entire inheritance and found himself homeless and starving. Out of desperation, the young son decided to return home and ask his father for a job.

What the young son did not anticipate was that his father anxiously watched for him, and the minute the son came into view, the father ran to him, threw his arms around him, and quickly celebrated him as a family member, not a servant. Although the young son tried to explain why he didn't deserve to be part of the family, the father did not even seem to hear him and threw a party to celebrate the return of his lost child. In this story, Jesus was illustrating for us the reality of the love of the Father, the One who anxiously waits for you and will continue to wait as long as it takes. He is loving to the point of sheer embarrassment. He will openly make a fool of himself and risk your rejection of him.

This is the Father who organized the adoption plan with the Son, who willingly carried it out, and with the Spirit, who agreed to help the Son and future adopted children. This is the depth of love that your God has for you. The Father, the Son, and the Spirit know everything about you, including every detail of who you are and what you have done. Their family system is full of love, encouragement, kindness, and respect. This is the family in which its members agree to sacrifice it all to save the one who is missing: you. Oh, you are so loved.

Bring It to Life

- Read Luke 15:11–32, the story that I summarized above. Take time to consider the heart and compassion of the father for both of his sons. What qualities or actions of the father stand out to you?

- People sometimes struggle to distinguish their earthly father from their heavenly Father. All earthly fathers are sinful; not one of them perfectly represents our heavenly Father. Has your view of your earthly father influenced your relationship with your heavenly Father? In what ways has it positively and/or negatively affected your relationship with God?

- How does the idea of God as family relate to your current experience of the word *family*?

To my Abba Father, Son, and the Spirit, I thank you for the deep love and devotion you have for me and am so amazed at the depth of your commitment to save me. I pray that I will have a new understanding of how badly you desire a relationship with me. I pray that my mind and heart will be transformed to see you as you are: one God in three persons, extending your infinite love to me. I pray that depression and anxiety will flee and be replaced with a deep comfort and peace that your love brings.

ACKNOWLEDGMENTS

God used countless people to make this project come to life.

To Steven Johnson with Five Stone Media for seeing the possibilities before I did, and to BroadStreet Publishing for providing this opportunity.

To my dear friends at Trinity Church in Lakeville, Minnesota, who provided continuous support and encouragement, especially the members of our small group. We couldn't have done it without you. Special thanks to the Bonnema family at the Echo Mountain Inn in Hendersonville, North Carolina, for hosting me through this project and becoming dear friends. Much love to you.

Thank you to the faculty and staff at Columbia International University, including Dr. Layman, Robertson McQuilken, Frank Bedell, and Steve Bradley. Dr. Beyer, thank you for your wisdom, your friendship, and your commitment to helping this book come to life.

Special thanks to the focus group: Lisa O'Leary, Nancy Roetman, Karl Watje, Danny Crompton, Valerie Beck, and Julie Hull. To Theresa Calsbeek, Anna Ganter, and DJ Blankenship-Kerby.

To my friend Colin Thornley, who has taught me so much about the gospel and the depth of Jesus' love for me. Thank you to Terri Hands, LMFT, my personal and professional mentor and friend. To Mark Anderson, LMFT, for investing in me and helping me grow as a therapist. .

Thank you, Galen and Teresa Watje (Dad and Mom), for your love of Jesus and your love for me. Your sacrificial love has given me a powerful understanding of God as a parent. To Carter, I don't have the words to tell you how much you have impacted my life, and I continue to learn from you. To Matthew, you are the gift we prayed so hard for, and your courage astounds me. I love you both. To Timmer, the love of my life and my best friend, I have no words to adequately describe my appreciation.

Thank you to Glen Bloomstrom for his tireless work in helping others. Your investment has greatly influenced my life and the lives of others.

Lastly, to my dear Pat Bradley: You were right all along.

REFERENCES

Abrams, Allison. "Shutting Down Body Shaming." *Psychology Today*, October 10, 2017. https://www.psychologytoday.com/us/blog/nurturing-self-compassion/201710/shutting-down-body-shaming.

Bekoff, Dr. Marc. "Why Sheep Matter: They're Intelligent, Emotional, and Unique." *Psychology Today*. Sussex Publishers, May 12, 2019. https://www.psychologytoday.com/us/blog/animal-emotions/201905/why-sheep-matter-theyre-intelligent-emotional-and-unique.

Brand, Chad, Eric Alan Mitchell, Steve Bonds, E. Ray Clendenen, Trent C. Butler, and Bill Latta. *Holman Illustrated Bible Dictionary*. Nashville, TN: Holman Reference, 2003.

Bromiley, G. W., Gerhard Friedrich, and Gerhard Kittel. *Theological Dictionary of the New Testament*. Translated by Geoffrey W. Bromiley. Vol. 3. Grand Rapids: MI: William B. Eerdmans, 1964.

Castaneda, Ruben. "How Your Secrets Can Damage and Maybe Even Kill You." *U.S. News & World Report*, June 26, 2017. https://health.usnews.com/wellness/mind/articles/2017-06-26/how-your-secrets-can-damage-and-maybe-even-kill-you.

Centers for Disease Control and Prevention. "Commercial Fishing Safety: Commercial Fishing in the United States." U.S. Department of Health and Human Services, June 25, 2019. https://www.cdc.gov/niosh/topics/fishing/nationaloverview.html.

Cherry, Katie E., Laura Sampson, Sandro Galea, Loren D. Marks, Pamela F. Nezat, Kayla H. Baudoin, and Bethany A. Lyon. "Optimism and Hope After Multiple Disasters: Relationships to Health-Related Quality of Life," *Journal of Loss and Trauma*. Vol. 22, no. 1 (2016): 61–76. https://doi.org/10.1080/15325024.2016.1187047.

Cohen, Lawrence J. *The Opposite of Worry: the Playful Parenting Approach to Childhood Anxieties and Fears*. New York: Ballantine Books, 2013.

Cooper, Carlotta. *The Complete Beginner's Guide to Raising Small Animals: Everything You Need to Know about Raising Cows, Sheep, Chickens, Ducks, Rabbits, and More*. Ocala, FL: Atlantic Publishing Group, Inc., 2012.

Cooper, Rodney L., and Max E. Anders. *Holman New Testament Commentary: Mark*. Nashville, TN: Holman Reference/B&H Publishing, 2000.

Cloud, Henry, and John Sims Townsend. *Safe People: How to Find Relationships That Are Good for You and Avoid Those That Aren't*. Grand Rapids, MI: Zondervan, 2016.

Crick, Julie "Wind Is Essential to Natural Processes." Michigan State University Extension. March 30, 2017. https://www.canr.msu.edu/news/wind_is_essential_to_natural_processes.

Cumming, Robert. *Great Artists Explained*. New York, NY: DK Publishers, 2007.

Easton, M. G. *Easton's Bible Dictionary*. New York NY: Harper & Brothers, 2001.

Eisenberger, N. I. "Does Rejection Hurt? An FMRI Study of Social Exclusion." *Science* vol. 302, no. 5643 (2003): 290–292. doi:10.1126/science.1089134.

Fitzpatrick, Elyse. *Home: How Heaven and the New Earth Satisfy Our Deepest Longings*. Minneapolis, MN: Bethany House Publishers, 2016.

Gilbert, Elizabeth T., and Melissa Gerber. *Color: a Practical Guide to Color and Its Uses in Art*. Lake Forest, CA: Walter Foster Publishing, 2017.

Gower, Ralph, and Fred Wight. *The New Manners and Customs of Bible Times*. Chicago: Moody Press, 1987.

Gundry, Robert H. *A Survey of the New Testament*. Grand Rapids, MI: Zondervan, 2012.

Grabe, S.; L. M. Ward, J. S. Hyde. "The Role of the Media in Body Image Concerns among Women: A Meta-Analysis of Experimental and Correlational Studies." *Psychological Bulletin* vol. 134, no. 3 (2008).

Green, Jay P. *Interlinear Greek-English New Testament,* 3rd edition. Grand Rapids, MI: Baker Books,1996.

Harris, R. Laird, Gleason L. Archer, and Bruce K. Waltke. *Theological Workbook of the Old Testament*. Vol. 2. Chicago: Moody Press, 1980.

Hasheider, Philip. *How to Raise Sheep: Everything You Need to Know*. Minneapolis, MN: Voyageur, 2014.

"Hunger Games: Do You Know Why You Eat?" Mayo Clinic. Mayo

Foundation for Medical Education and Research, May 22, 2019. https://www.mayoclinic.org/healthy-lifestyle/weight-loss/in-depth/hunger-games-do-you-know-why-you-eat/art-20342120.

Jacob, Dr. Jacquie. "Normal Behaviors of Chickens in Small and Backyard Poultry Flocks." *Small and Backyard Poultry*. University of Kentucky. poultry.extension.org/articles/poultry-behavior/normal-behaviors-of-chickens-in-small-and-backyard-poultry-flocks/.

Kaufmann, Martina, and Roland Neumann. "The Effects of Priming Subjective Control on Reports of Fear." *Motivation and Emotion* vol. 43, no. 5 (2019): 814–823. https://doi.org/10.1007/s11031-019-09763-z.

Keller, Tim, and Kathy Keller. "How the Psalms Are Actually Songs of Jesus." *Crosswalk.com* (blog), November 19, 2015. https://www.crosswalk.com/faith/bible-study/how-the-psalms-are-actually-songs-of-jesus.html.

Koplos, Janet. *What Makes a Potter: Functional Pottery in America Today*. Atglen, PA: Schiffer Publishing, 2019.

Keil, C. F., F. Delitzsch. *Commentary on the Old Testament*. Peabody, Massachusetts: Hendrickson Publishers, 1996.

Levitin, Dr. Daniel. "Speaking of Psychology: Music and Your Health." American Psychological Association, October 11, 2020. https://www.apa.org/research/action/speaking-of-psychology/music-health.

McAndrew, Frank. "The Perils of Social Isolation." *Psychology Today*, November 12, 2016. https://www.psychologytoday.com/us/blog/out-the-ooze/201611/the-perils-social-isolation.

Merriam-Webster's Collegiate Dictionary. 11th ed. Springfield, MA: Merriam-Webster, 2003. Continually updated at https://www.merriam-webster.com/.

Owings, Lisa. *The African Lion*. Minneapolis, MN: Bellwether Media, 2012.

Watje, Captain Karl J., USMC. Interviewed by Jenita Pace. October 6, 2020.

Phillips, John. *Exploring the Psalms*. Neptune, NJ: Loizeaux Brothers, 1988.

Piper, John. "A Brief Theology of Sleep." *Desiring God* (website). August 3, 1982. https://www.desiringgod.org/articles/a-brief-theology-of-sleep.

Seymore, Simon. *Big Cats*. New York, NY: Harper Collins, 2017.

Shedler, Dr. Jonathan. "Getting to Know Me: What's Behind Psychoanalysis." *Scientific American Mind*, November 2010. https://www.scientificamerican.com/article/getting-to-know-me/.

"Sleep Deprivation and Deficiency." National Heart Lung and Blood Institute. U.S. Department of Health and Human Services, https://www.nhlbi.nih.gov/health-topics/sleep-deprivation-and-deficiency.

Sproul, R. C. *A Walk with God: Luke*. Fearn, Ross-shire, Scotland: Christian Focus Publications, 2011.

Sproul, R. C. *Who Is Jesus?* Lake Mary, FL: Reform Trust Publishing, 2009.

Strong, James. *Strong's Exhaustive Concordance of the Bible*. Peabody, MA: Hendrickson Publishers, 1940.

The New Strong's Concise Dictionary of Bible Words. Nashville, TN: Thomas Nelson Publishers, 2000.

The Lexham Bible Dictionary. J. D. Barry and L. Wentz, editors. Bellingham, WA: Lexham Press, 2012. As found in the Logos Bible study software program.

Thomson, Helen. "When the Best Is Not Enough." *New Scientist* 243, no. 3243 (2019): 35–37. https://doi.org/10.1016/s0262-4079(19)31536-2.

Tinker, Ben, and Dr. Matthew Sleeth. "The Importance of a 'Stop Day.'" CNN, January 11, 2013. https://www.cnn.com/2013/01/11/health/sleeth-take-day-off/index.html.

Vine, W. E., William White, Jr, and Merrill Unger. *Vine's Complete Expository Dictionary of Old and New Testament Words*. Nashville, TN: Thomas Nelson, 1984.

Weir, Kirsten. "The Pain of Social Rejection." *Monitor on Psychology*. American Psychological Association, 2012. https://www.apa.org/monitor/2012/04/rejection.

Wells, Dr. Tara. "Dealing with Disappointment." *Psychology Today*, June 25, 2017. https://www.psychologytoday.com/us/blog/the-clarity/201706/dealing-disappointment.

Zamek, Jeff. *The Ceramics Studio Guide: What Potters Should Know*. Atglen, PA: Schiffer Publishing Ltd., 2019.

ENDNOTES

1 Carlotta Cooper, *The Complete Beginner's Guide to Raising Small Animals: Everything You Need to Know about Raising Cows, Sheep, Chickens, Ducks, Rabbits, and More* (Ocala, FL: Atlantic Publishing Group, Inc., 2012), 288.

2 Philip Hasheider, *How to Raise Sheep: Everything You Need to Know* (Minneapolis, MN: Voyageur, 2014), 91.

3 Dr. Marc Bekoff, "Why Sheep Matter: They're Intelligent, Emotional, and Unique," *Psychology Today*, May 12, 2019, https://www.psychologytoday.com/us/blog/animal-emotions/201905/why-sheep-matter-theyre-intelligent-emotional-and-unique.

4 Ralph Gower and Fred Wight, *The New Manners and Customs of Bible Times* (Chicago: Moody Press, 1987), 135–136.

5 Gower, *The New Manners*, 140.

6 Gower, *The New Manners*, 138.

7 Carlotta Cooper, *Raising Small Animals*, 288.

8 Gower, *The New Manners*, 136.

9 Lisa Owings, *The African Lion* (Minneapolis, MN: Bellwether Media, 2012), 10.

10 Simon Seymore, *Big Cats* (New York, NY: Harper Collins, 2017), 19–22.

11 Seymore, *Big Cats*, 10.

12 Seymore, *Big Cats*, 19.

13 Martina Kaufmann and Roland Neumann, "The Effects of Priming Subjective Control on Reports of Fear," *Motivation and Emotion*, vol. 43, no. 5 (2019), 814–23. https://doi.org/10.1007/s11031-019-09763-z.

14 Helen Thomson, "When the Best Is Not Enough," *New Scientist* vol. 243, no. 3243 (2019), 35–37, https://doi.org/10.1016/s0262-4079(19)31536-2.

15 R. C. Sproul, *A Walk with God: Luke* (Fearn, Ross-shire, Scotland: Christian Focus Publications, 2011), 5.

16 Rodney L. Cooper and Max E. Anders, *Holman New Testament Commentary: Mark* (Nashville, TN: Holman Reference/B&H Publishing, 2000), 5.

17 American Counseling Association, *ACA Code of Ethics*, page 4, Revised 2014, https://www.counseling.org/Resources/aca-code-of-ethics.pdf.

18 ACA, *Code of Ethics*, 4, 5, 9.

19 Dr. Jonathan Shedler, "Getting to Know Me: What's Behind Psychoanalysis." *Scientific American Mind*, November 2010, https://www.scientificamerican.com/article/getting-to-know-me/.

20 Shedler, "Getting to Know Me," 55.

21 Shedler, "Getting to Know Me," 55.

22 *Merriam-Webster.com Dictionary*, s.v. "redeem," accessed May 14, 2021, https://www.merriam-webster.com/dictionary/redeem.

23 Rodney L. Cooper and Max E. Anders, *Holman New Testament Commentary: Mark* (Nashville: Holman Reference/B&H Publishing, 2000), 42.

24 American Medical Association, "Patient-Physician Relationships, Opinion I.I.I," *Code of Medical Ethics*, https://www.ama-assn.org/delivering-care/ethics/patient-physician-relationships.

25 Frank McAndrew, "The Perils of Social Isolation," *Psychology Today*, November 12, 2016, https://www.psychologytoday.com/us/blog/out-the-ooze/201611/the-perils-social-isolation.

26 Robert H. Gundry, *A Survey of the New Testament* (Grand Rapids, MI: Zondervan, 2012), 134.

27 Jay P. Green, Sr., *Interlinear Greek-English New Testament*, 3rd ed. (Grand Rapids, MI: Baker Books, 1996).

28 Gower, *The New Manners*, 153–155.

29 R.C. Sproul, *Who Is Jesus?* (Lake Mary, FL: Reform Trust Publishing, 2009).

30 Dr. Tara Wells, "Dealing with Disappointment," *Psychology Today*, June 25, 2017, https://www.psychologytoday.com/us/blog/the-clarity/201706/dealing-disappointment.

31 N. I. Eisenberger, "Does Rejection Hurt? An FMRI Study of Social Exclusion," *Science*, vol. 302, no. 5643 (2003): 290–292, https://science.sciencemag.org/content/302/5643/290.

32 Kirsten Weir, "The Pain of Social Rejection," *Monitor on Psychology*, American Psychological Association, vol. 43, no. 4 (2012): 50, https://www.apa.org/monitor/2012/04/rejection.

33 *Merriam-Webster.com Dictionary*, s.v. "bridge," accessed May 15, 2021, https://www.merriam-webster.com/dictionary/bridge.

34 Julie Crick, "Wind Is Essential to Natural Processes," Michigan

State University Extension, March 30, 2017, https://www.canr.msu.edu/news/wind_is_essential_to_natural_processes.

35 James Strong, "pnuema," *Strong's Exhaustive Concordance of the Bible,* in the Greek dictionary (Peabody, MA: Hendrickson Publishers, 1940), no. 4151, p. 58. 1.

36 Tim Keller and Kathy Keller, "How the Psalms Are Actually Songs of Jesus," *Crosswalk.com* (blog), November 19, 2015, https://www.crosswalk.com/faith/bible-study/how-the-psalms-are-actually-songs-of-jesus.html.

37 Dr. Daniel Levitin, "Speaking of Psychology: Music and Your Health," American Psychological Association, October 11, 2020, https://www.apa.org/research/action/speaking-of-psychology/music-health.

38 Robert Cumming, *Great Artists Explained* (New York, NY: DK Publishing, 2007), 6.

39 Elizabeth T. Gilbert and Melissa Gerber, *Color: A Practical Guide to Color and Its Uses in Art* (Lake Forest, CA: Walter Foster Publishing, 2017), 25–26.

40 Centers for Disease Control and Prevention, "Commercial Fishing Safety: Commercial Fishing in the United States," U.S. Department of Health and Human Services, June 25, 2019, https://www.cdc.gov/niosh/topics/fishing/nationaloverview.html.

41 Ben Tinker, "The Importance of a 'Stop Day,'" CNN, A Warner Media Company, January 11, 2013, https://www.cnn.com/2013/01/11/health/sleeth-take-day-off/index.html.

42 Tinker, "The Importance of a 'Stop Day.'"

43 John Piper, "A Brief Theology of Sleep," *Desiring God* (website), August 3, 1982, https://www.desiringgod.org/articles/a-brief-theology-of-sleep.

44 "Sleep Deprivation and Deficiency," National Heart, Lung, and Blood Institute, U.S. Department of Health and Human Services, accessed on May 16, 2021, https://www.nhlbi.nih.gov/health-topics/sleep-deprivation-and-deficiency.

45 "Sleep Deprivation and Deficiency," National Heart, Lung, and Blood Institute.

46 W. E. Vine, William White, Jr., and Merrill Unger, "Shield," *Vine's Complete Expository Dictionary of Old and New Testament Words* (Nashville, TN: Thomas Nelson, 1984), 571.

47 John Phillips, *Exploring the Psalms* (Neptune, New Jersey: Loizeaux Brothers, 1988), 695.

48 Lawrence J. Cohen, *The Opposite of Worry: the Playful Parenting Approach to Childhood Anxieties and Fears* (New York, NY: Ballantine Books, 2013), 11–12.

49 Captain Karl J. Watje, USMC, interview with Jenita Pace, October 6, 2020.

50 Watje, interview with Jenita Pace.

51 "Hunger Games: Do You Know Why You Eat?" Mayo Clinic, Mayo Foundation for Medical Education and Research, May 22, 2019, https://www.mayoclinic.org/healthy-lifestyle/weight-loss/in-depth/hunger-games-do-you-know-why-you-eat/art-20342120.

52 Janet Koplos, *What Makes a Potter: Functional Pottery in America Today* (Atglen, PA: Schiffer Publishing, Ltd., 2019), 8.

53 Jeff Zamek, *The Ceramics Studio Guide: What Potters Should Know* (Atglen, PA: Schiffer Publishing, Ltd., 2019), 20–22.

54 Zamek, *The Ceramics Studio Guide*, 184–199.

55 Koplos, *What Makes a Potter*, 6.

56 Allison Abrams, "Shutting Down Body Shaming," *Psychology Today*, October 10, 2017, https://www.psychologytoday.com/us/blog/nurturing-self-compassion/201710/shutting-down-body-shaming.

57 Grabe, S.; L. M. Ward, J. S. Hyde. "The Role of the Media in Body Image Concerns among Women: A Meta-Analysis of Experimental and Correlational Studies," *Psychological Bulletin* vol. 134, no. 3 (2008).

58 Elyse Fitzpatrick, *Home: How Heaven and the New Earth Satisfy Our Deepest Longings* (Minneapolis, MN: Bethany House Publishers, 2016), 96.

59 Ruben Castaneda, "How Your Secrets Can Damage and Maybe Even Kill You," *U.S. News & World Report*, June 26, 2017, https://health.usnews.com/wellness/mind/articles/2017-06-26/how-your-secrets-can-damage-and-maybe-even-kill-you.

60 Castaneda, "How Your Secrets Can Damage."

61 Henry Cloud and John Sims Townsend, *Safe People: How to Find Relationships That Are Good for You and Avoid Those That Aren't* (Grand Rapids, MI: Zondervan, 2016), 21–24.

62 Cloud, *Safe People*, 164–165.

63 C. F. Keil and F. Delitzsch, *Commentary on the Old Testament* (Peabody, Massachusetts: Hendrickson Publishers, 1996), 137.

64 James Strong, "Rock," *The New Strong's Concise Dictionary of Bible Words* (Nashville, TN: Thomas Nelson Publishers, 2000), 99, 850.

65 Harris, R. Laird, Gleason L. Archer, and Bruce K. Waltke. *Theological Workbook of the Old Testament.* Vol. 2. (Chicago: Moody Press, 1980), 762.

66 James Strong, "Rock," *The New Strong's Concise Dictionary of Bible Words,* (Nashville, TN: Thomas Nelson Publishers, 2000), 99, 850.

67 Strong, *Dictionary of Bible Words,* 99, 850.

68 M. G. Easton, "Priest," *Easton's Bible Dictionary* (New York, NY: Harper & Brothers, 2001).

69 Dr. Jacquie Jacob, "Normal Behaviors of Chickens in Small and Backyard Poultry Flocks," *Small and Backyard Poultry,* University of Kentucky, accessed May 18, 2021, poultry.extension.org/articles/poultry-behavior/normal-behaviors-of-chickens-in-small-and-backyard-poultry-flocks/.

70 J. D. Barry and L. Wentz, eds., "temple," subheading under "the second temple," *The Lexham Bible Dictionary* (Bellingham, WA: Lexham Press, 2012), as found in the Logos Bible Software program.

71 Katie E. Cherry, Laura Sampson, et al., "Optimism and Hope After Multiple Disasters: Relationships to Health-Related Quality of Life," *Journal of Loss and Trauma,* vol. 22, no. 1 (2016): 61–76, https://doi.org/10.1080/15325024.2016.1187047.

72 Easton, "Abba," *Easton's Bible Dictionary.*

ABOUT THE AUTHOR

Jenita is a licensed counselor in the state of Minnesota. She received a bachelor's degree in Bible and humanities from Columbia International University in 2004 and a master's in education in school counseling from Western Carolina University in 2013. Jenita spent the early part of her career working with teenagers in various schools in North Carolina before moving back to her home state of Minnesota and starting her own private practice, called Three Rivers Counseling. In addition, she is an adjunct professor for Northwestern University in St. Paul, Minnesota.

Jenita Pace and her husband, Tim, have two sons, Carter and Matthew, and a sheepadoodle named Charlotte. They currently reside in Bloomington, Minnesota. Jenita enjoys horseback riding, playing board games, and chasing her kids around the house. It's not uncommon for her to throw themed parties for her friends and family, and she enjoys being creative in finding ways to make them laugh.

Jenita and Tim have been involved in various film projects, podcasts, and speaking engagements that provide awareness and support for couples who are struggling with depression and anxiety. She has also been a guest speaker and trainer for various ministries and churches.

For more information on how to connect with Jenita, as well as additional resources available, visit her website at www.threeriversmn.com.